BE *Still*

BE *Still*

USING PRINCIPLES OF THE GOSPEL
TO LOWER ANXIETY

G. SHELDON
MARTIN

Covenant Communications, Inc.

Published by Covenant Communications, Inc.
American Fork, Utah

Printed in the United States of America
First Printing: January 2013

19 18 17 16 15 14 13   10 9 8 7 6 5 4 3 2 1

ISBN-13: 978-1-62108-318-4

I dedicate this book to my loving wife, Nicole, who supports me in all of my endeavors. Nicole, you are the best wife a husband could ever dream of having.

Acknowledgments

Special thanks to Christy Hardman, Miriam Pethel, and Jay Martin for their transcription, grammar, content, and feedback contributions. Special thanks to Samantha Millburn and the rest of the Covenant staff for their hours of help on this project.

Introduction

I SEE SO MANY PEOPLE every year who feel worthless, useless, or frustrated with the direction they're going. The irony is, many of them are doing everything they are "supposed" to do. So if they're doing everything right, why do they feel this way?

I write to the individual who feels they are never good enough, the person who feels that no matter how hard they try, they will never measure up. I write to the individual who knows that the Atonement has the ability to heal but lacks the confidence that it can help them personally.

I once met with a wonderful woman in therapy who harbored these exact feelings. She tried so hard to do everything she was supposed to do, but she worried excessively about her own salvation, the approval of others, her inabilities, and her worth.

One day she broke down crying and said, "Sheldon, why do I feel this way? Why do I feel that I will never be good enough? Why do I not like myself?"

Obviously, these questions can't be answered in a short two-paragraph answer, but let me share an observation I made about this sister.

She could raise her hand in Sunday School and answer every gospel question the teachers asked. She knew the "answers," but she did not *believe* and *process* the answers. Thoughts lead to feelings. If we process distorted or incorrect thoughts, those thoughts will lead to negative feelings. If we repeat a thought pattern enough times, the process becomes almost automatic.

I have met with hundreds of clients who process thoughts that lead to anxiety. I do not claim that this book is a cure-all for anxiety, but learning to confront, challenge, and modify thoughts is essential for anyone trying to work through excessive worry.

In referring to the term *anxiety*, I want to be cautious that we do not get the wrong idea. Actually, anxiety is often used in a positive form in the scriptures. The Doctrine and Covenants says we should be "*anxiously engaged* in a good cause" (D&C 58:27; emphasis added). There is a level of anxiety that is healthy, required, and important for us. However, in this book, whenever I use the word *anxiety*, I will use it in the context of *excessive* worry—too much worry.

One of the main sources of anxiety stems from repeated irrational or incorrect thoughts. If we process thoughts that are incorrect, we will often feel an increase of worry.

THE WAY THE MIND WORKS

Our minds continually create patterns that become automatic. While many patterns are healthy and helpful, some are not. The process of undoing a pattern does not happen by accident. An individual must confront the incorrect thought, challenge it, and then modify that thought so it is correct.

Many individuals feel that too much worry or anxiety comes from a situation in their lives. This is not accurate. To illustrate this concept, think of the following example. How would you feel if you received a C+ on an assignment? You may feel sad, depressed, down, upset, or even suicidal. Or you may feel happy, excited, ecstatic, and elated. We learn something important from this example—the event did not cause the feeling; the interpretation, thought, or perception of the event caused the feeling.

Just as thoughts lead to actions, they also lead to feelings. President Boyd K. Packer said, "True doctrine, understood, changes attitudes and behavior."[1] I want to focus on the word *understood*. A lot of the principles we cover in this book will not be new to you; most LDS people have heard them. They can even quote these principles in Sunday School—but they struggle to apply them. I feel it is different to be able to raise our hand and quote a principle than it is to truly understand, believe, and *live* a principle. If we want the doctrine to change us, we must understand it, process it, and rely on it.

If we process distorted facts repeatedly, we will probably experience an increase of anxiety. When we process correct thoughts, it often naturally reduces our anxiety.

Often, when someone is trying to get rid of an anxious thought, they will force themselves to try not to think about it. Unfortunately, the brain does not work this way. For example, for the next thirty seconds, try your hardest not to think about pink elephants. Don't think about them dancing or running or playing ping-pong or doing anything at all. You are absolutely *not* to think about pink elephants.

You see? It's almost impossible to do.

The reason this happens is that our brain does not effectively distinguish between "think about" and "don't think about." When people get a little anxious about something and their brain starts processing a thought, they may even tell themselves, "Don't think about this, and don't think about that," but they start to feel worse. It's because that thought process actually increases anxiety.

Here's the trick, and it gives us a little bit of a framework. Do not think about a pink elephant—think about a brown monkey instead. When I ask people, "What are you thinking about now?" they'll often say, "A brown monkey." The reason is this: the best way to get rid of a thought we don't want to think about is to replace it with a new thought.

This is the framework we will use throughout this book. I will present situations I've seen many times in counseling. We will identify the distorted thought (pink elephant) and focus on correct principles (brown monkey).

It is important to understand that this process will not happen by accident. The framework is simple, and to some it may seem like it's too simple to work. Remember, knowing what to do and doing it are two entirely different things. How many people *know* how to lose weight compared to the number who actually do it?

I challenge you to keep an open mind and believe that if you can identify and modify incorrect thoughts and learn to turn your thoughts to the Savior, then, by the power of the Atonement, your thought processes *can* align with real truth, where there is no worry or fear, only peace through the grace of Him who can save us all.

We have many scriptural examples of prophets confronting and modifying a thought. One of my favorites is in Alma 36, where Alma the Elder is recounting his story to his son. Pay close attention to the words he uses, and keep in mind this concept of confronting a thought and replacing it with a new thought.

Alma says, "And it came to pass that as I was thus racked with torment, while I was harrowed up by the memory of my many sins, behold, I remembered also to have heard my father prophesy unto the people concerning the coming of one Jesus Christ, a Son of God, to atone for the sins of the world. Now, as my mind caught hold upon this *thought*, I cried within my heart: O Jesus, thou Son of God, have mercy on me, who am in the gall of bitterness, and am encircled about by the everlasting chains of death" (Alma 36:17–18; emphasis added).

Notice what Alma does in this experience. When he is thinking about his sins, he feels "racked" and "tormented." Then his mind catches hold of a new thought, the greatest thought we can have—the Atonement. And he begins to process thoughts like, "I can be forgiven," "I can be washed clean." And then, when his mind catches "hold upon *this thought*," he cries within his heart, "O Jesus, thou Son of God, have mercy on me" (Alma 36:18; emphasis added).

Another example is when Satan comes to tempt Moses. Notice what Moses does; I think it is a similar framework here. "And it came to pass that when Moses had said these words, behold, Satan came tempting him, saying: Moses, son of man, worship me. And it came to pass that Moses looked upon Satan and said: Who art thou? For behold, I am a son of God, in the similitude of his Only Begotten" (Moses 1:12–13).

If Moses would have looked hard enough for evidence that he was a "son of man," as Satan suggested, he would have found it pretty easily and maybe would have begun to believe what the adversary was saying. Instead, in that moment, Moses processed the thought, "I am a son of God," and as he did that over and over, Moses came off conqueror.

So our goal is to identify distorted thoughts, learn to replace them with correct thoughts, and then practice this over and over and over again. The key ingredient in changing a thought pattern is consistency. Repetition must be present for an automatic thought pattern to occur.

We can practice through writing in a journal, pondering, discussing, studying the scriptures, and visualizing. There are many ways to process these correct thoughts, but we must do it over and over again. The more often we do it, the more successful we are going to be.

I want to begin with testifying that I know that when we treasure up true gospel principles in our hearts and minds, we feel more peace. I know the Savior is the only one who can offer the peace we all seek. He will reign one day on this earth as King of Kings and Lord of Lords. He is the Prince of Peace. He is not just the Prince of Peace for the calamities of earth but also for the calamities of every troubled heart. May we turn to Him and His teachings. His gospel heals the wounded soul and calms the troubled heart. I know this to be true and have seen it countless times.

Principle 1 –
We Can Be Purified and Cleansed through the Sacrament

SITUATION

A young mother comes into my office and says, "I can't do it anymore. I yell at my kids constantly. I'm not who I'm supposed to be. I'm supposed to read my scriptures every day, but I can't find the time. I get frustrated with the sisters in the ward. Why try? I can't do it anymore."

> *Distorted Thought: Either I am totally perfect and adequate in every single way, or I'm a failure.*

This thought is *not* true. It's a distorted thought. If you were to ask everyone on planet earth to identify something they would like to improve in themselves, close to 100 percent would be able to identify something they want to work on. If anyone stood up and said, "Nope, I don't think I have anything to improve," we might have other issues with that person.

If you, like everyone else, have something you need to improve in yourself and you are processing the thought that you either have to be completely perfect or you are a failure, then you are building a framework that will lead only to frustration.

The Lord "cannot look upon sin with the least degree of allowance" (D&C 1:31), so I am not suggesting that we need to be okay with our shortcomings and not bother to work on them. There has been only One in all of history who went through mortality perfectly. If you can't recognize, remember, and apply that true thought, you will deny one of the truths of mortality: we sin, and without the Atonement we are lost. It is important to recognize that this is not just a phrase we say in Sunday School to get the "right" answer. We *are* going to sin, come up short, and demonstrate weakness in this life. Instead of using this information to give us allowance to sin, we should use this information to draw us closer to the Lord and His majestic Atonement.

I meet with many individuals who have convinced themselves that the cure for their life is to never make another mistake. The reason they become frustrated is they are reminded on a daily basis of their shortcomings. Somehow, these individuals feel they should float through mortality without making any mistakes or misjudgments. This is completely unrealistic and distorted.

Fortunately, there are some solutions to these feelings of "never being good enough." When we feel overwhelmed by our weaknesses and shortcomings, the sacrament can give us comfort and courage. It is designed to be a purifying ordinance that allows us to begin anew on a consistent basis.

President Henry B. Eyring said, "We have great helps to give us courage in this life. The greatest is the Atonement of Jesus Christ. Because of what he did, sins can be washed away in the waters of baptism."

Now pay attention to this next part of the quote, and remember, he's talking about our sins being washed away: "We can renew that blessing when we partake of the Sacrament in faith and with a repentant heart."[2]

President Eyring reminds us that when we worthily partake of the sacrament, it should give us courage to try again, because if we have repented, our sins are *washed away*.

In *True to the Faith*, under "Sacrament," it says, "In partaking of the sacrament and making these commitments, you renew your baptismal covenant. You receive great blessings when you keep the baptismal covenant. As you renew it, the *Lord renews the promised remission of your sins*."[3]

What a wonderful thought! If we come to the sacrament table with a repentant heart, with real intent and feeling, which means we want to improve and do better, the Lord will renew His promised blessing of the sacrament—a remission of our sins. So though we cannot be perfect or sinless every single day of our lives, God has given us a means to start our perfection process anew each week. We cannot be perfect every moment of every day, but we can keep trying through the Atonement.

Elder Dallin H. Oaks says, "Baptism is for the remission of sins. And the sacrament is a renewal of the covenant and *blessings* of baptism. Both should be preceded by repentance."[4]

Elder L. Tom Perry has also repeated this message: "As we worthily partake of the sacrament, we witness that we are willing to take the Savior's name upon us and keep His commandments and *do* always remember Him, that we may have His Spirit to be with us. In this way the covenant of our *baptism is renewed.*"⁵

It may seem repetitive to cite so many similar quotes, but I include all of them because I meet with dozens of Church members who do not believe they can begin anew on a regular basis. They may say they *believe* this doctrine, but their actions speak louder than their words. Something as simple as partaking of the sacrament worthily with a desire to change and improve and then talking to the bishop after church about past sins as a youth demonstrates that a person does not truly believe in the covenants they have made and the promises that attend those covenants.

I know that many of us, if not all of us, have times when we feel overwhelmed. I'm encouraged when I read in the scriptures that prophets were overwhelmed at times too. They felt they didn't speak well enough or weren't prepared or weren't sure how they were going to accomplish the task the Lord had given them. Their examples can help us understand that the Lord has given us a way to begin anew on a regular basis, because if someone like Nephi felt like a "wretched man" and became who we know Nephi became, we can have the courage to believe that we can progress as well. If Enoch, who felt he was not qualified for the job, did what he did, we can have courage that the Lord can take us from where we are to higher ground. If the Lord can take an uneducated farm boy like Joseph Smith and help him do what he did, then He can do something for us as well.

Throughout the growth process for Nephi, Enoch, and Joseph, they must have had moments of wiping the slate clean and starting again. To think that we can start anew gives us courage. Listen to the words of Nephi: "O wretched man that I am! Yea, my heart sorroweth because of my flesh; my soul grieveth because of mine iniquities. I am encompassed about because of the temptations and the sins which do easily beset me . . . nevertheless, I know in whom I have trusted" (2 Nephi 4:17–19). Nephi felt inadequate and sinful but replaced his negative thoughts with the memory that he had trusted in the Lord and in His promised blessings. We too can trust that our overwhelming burdens can be covered by the Atonement of Jesus Christ. We are not stuck with the situation we are in forever, and we do not need to have continual negative feelings. We can remember that we trust Christ; we trust Him to help us become a little better and endure a little more.

One Possible Correct Thought

The Lord, in His great mercy, will allow me to be cleansed and start again next Sunday. When we start to feel overwhelmed and feel our shortcomings wash over us in great waves—when we feel we just can't go on because if we're not totally good, then we must be bad—then we must realize we can start over.

I know that when I process that thought, I take the sacrament differently. I sing the sacrament hymns differently. I stand all amazed at the great love Jesus constantly offers me. How wonderful, beautiful, and significant it is that the Lord has designed a way for us to begin anew on a regular basis.

Helpful Application Activity

Replacing and substituting a thought is often easier said than done. The act of replacing a thought and ultimately changing a thought pattern takes consistency. *Through small and simple things, great things come to pass* (see Alma 37:6–7).

Get a journal you can write in specifically for these exercises. Remember, this does not have to be a journal to pass on to the grandkids someday. I would rather you be honest and throw it away than be fake and not change.

Writing is the most refined way to process a thought as you move toward changing a thought pattern. When you feel overwhelmed, answer these two questions in your "thoughts and feelings" journal:

1. What feelings and thoughts are making me feel overwhelmed?
2. What principles of the gospel can help me modify my thoughts correctly?

Example:

Feelings and thoughts making me feel overwhelmed	Principles of the gospel that can help me modify my thoughts
I feel I am a bad father because I do not spend enough time with the kids.	I am trying to do my best. No, I haven't spent a significant amount of time with them, but I have spent as much time as my schedule would allow this week. And maybe next week I can spend more time. The Lord, in His goodness, will forgive me, purify me, and let me try again.

I feel if I were more competent, I would have taught better on Sunday.	I may not be a gospel scholar, but I did prepare as much as I could for my lesson. I can take the sacrament and begin anew, and next time, I will pray for more direction as I teach my class.
I yelled at the kids today and feel like a bad mother. I wish I would stop doing that.	True, I should not yell at the kids; however, I am doing much better, and I can be purified, move forward, and continue to improve.

Principle 2 —

We Cannot Change the Past, No Matter How Much We Worry about It

We must learn to focus on the direction we are headed. When I say we can't change the past, I'm not referring to the process of repentance. The Lord says He remembers our sins no more when we properly repent (see D&C 58:42–43), and we need to trust in that promise. So when I say we can't change the past, I am referring to actually going into the past with a time machine and changing an event we wish we could change. No one can rationally believe they can go into the past and literally change something, but many people emotionally return to the past, *wishing* they could change it. Let me give you some examples.

SITUATION

A father comes into my office and says, "You know, when I was twenty-one, I wish I would have . . ." Fill in the blank: I wish I would have majored in something different. I wish I would have gotten a different job. I wish I would have invested in successful companies. I wish I would have made better financial decisions. And on and on with these situations where they feel, "Oh, if I could just go into the past and do this differently, everything would be better."

Distorted Thought: Worrying about the past will change it.

What is distorted about this thought?

It's as if we think if we worry enough about the past it will change and we will feel loads better. We feel there is a threshold of worrying enough that all of a sudden the problem will go away and be replaced with peace.

Do you see why this is distorted? Worrying about the past is an absolute waste of emotional energy. Consider the reality of the amount of time wasted worrying about something we cannot control. It's like worrying about gravity or the weather. The amount of time we spend worrying has no effect on the outcome.

I had a professor in graduate school who, during the class, started laying out a situation he would have done differently. He laid out a foolproof plan of how he would have majored a little bit differently and just at the right time. He would have gotten a different master's degree and then moved on to a PhD. If he would have made these changes, his current situation would have been professionally flawless. This professor was trying to emphasize to the class that if he would have received a second master's degree in nursing, he could have prescribed medication and competed with psychiatrists.

Here is why I think this is so irrational: He knew his plan was a good decision only because of the life he had lived. He had no idea as a freshman in college that laws were going to be changed ten years down the road and that if he had majored in something different he would have been able to do a lot more with his graduate degree.

I once met with a man who said, "If I had it to do over again, I'd invest all my money in Microsoft when it was a brand-new company." But he knew that was a good decision only because he'd seen what had happened since then.

We need to give ourselves a little bit of a break. I think most people can look at their lives and realize they could have made better decisions, but many times we make the best decision we know how in that moment.

Are all decisions right? No. In fact, many of them are wrong. That is part of mortality; it's part of growing up; it's part of what we do as fallible mortal beings. We make mistakes and incorrect decisions. That's how we learn.

Elder M. Russell Ballard gave us clear direction about what to do when we make mistakes. He said, "You must clear the problem up and then not spend one more second worrying about it. Past problems are like a stream when you are standing on a bridge—the stream is rolling underneath you, and your problems have gone downstream. *Regardless of how hard you try, you cannot change the past.* What I want you to learn to do is to look upstream. Watch for the things that are coming down the river of life that you can change and control."[6]

What an encouraging thought. We need to look at our current lives and the things coming down the stream of life. We must recognize that if we continue to worry about past "wrong decisions," we are going to miss future opportunities coming down the stream of life.

Harold Hill, in the musical production *The Music Man*, said, "Live only for tomorrow, and you'll have a lot of empty yesterdays today."[7] Isn't that a great thought? I meet a lot of clients who say, "Sheldon, here's the deal. I made a mistake." And I'm not just talking about sin, although sin can apply in this example. I am mainly referring to people who will come in and say things like, "I wish I wouldn't have pulled out my 401K at that time." "I really wish I hadn't bought a house when the market was high," or "I wish I would have gone to law school," or "I wish I would have enjoyed college more and not rushed through it."

I'm guessing that when these individuals made those particular decisions, they thought they were pretty good ideas. The more often they look to the past and fantasize about making different choices, the more empty yesterdays they will have.

I met with a client one time who was retired and who was having a very difficult time emotionally. He kept saying, "I wish I would have had a different profession." I felt sad about his regrets. This was a good man, and yet, he was spending years of his life wishing he could go back to his early twenties to make a different decision.

In Luke 9:62, the Savior said, "No man, having put his hand to the plough, and looking back, is fit for the kingdom of God." That is strong language from the Savior. The Master of all analogies uses a plough to help us understand this concept.

I am not a very good farmer; in fact, I'm not even much of a gardener. I was excited because last year we actually cleared a spot to have a garden, but then I ended up spraying weed killer all over it because the weeds were so out of control. But I have used a tiller or plough before, and I know that if you try to plough looking backward, all it does is affect where you're headed. When you look back, you will recognize how crooked the path has been, but looking back affects your forward direction.

Think of that analogy when the Savior says—again, this is strong language—that no man having put his hand to the plough and looking back *is fit for the kingdom of God*.

I think that is a very important principle to process in our thoughts. The Lord is focused on the direction He wants us to head. He wants us to concentrate on progression.

Obviously, if there are things we need to clear up, we need to do that. But it sounds as if the Savior wants us to grab the plough, look forward, and start driving.

Do you remember the story of the woman taken in adultery? What direction does the Lord want the woman to go? "When Jesus had lifted up himself, and saw none but the woman, he said unto her, Woman, where are those thine accusers? hath no man condemned thee? She said, No man, Lord. And Jesus said unto her, *Neither do I condemn thee: go, and sin no more*" (John 8:10–11).

For me, that last verse screams direction. It does not justify or even rationalize the sin of adultery, but the focus seems to be that her direction should be different.

One of the many lessons we can learn from this story is that the Savior wants this woman to grab the plough and start changing for the future, to start driving forward. Many times, I find individuals in my office who can raise their hands in Sunday School and say they know the Lord forgives people, that no one is perfect, and that we've all made incorrect decisions. But they have a difficult time believing God has forgiven *them* and allowed *them* to focus on a new direction.

I mentioned earlier that this particular distorted thought is not just referring to sin. It can also refer to an individual who has properly repented but cannot forgive himself. The person replays the past constantly, wishing they could somehow go back and change it. This situation becomes tragic because the individual is denying the Atonement of Jesus Christ. He knows "people" can be forgiven, but he does not believe "he" can be forgiven.

One of the greatest quotes I've ever heard for this situation was given by Elder Richard G. Scott in a general conference. He said, "I testify that when a bishop or stake president has confirmed that your repentance is sufficient, know that your obedience has allowed the Atonement of Jesus Christ to satisfy the demands of justice for the laws you have broken. Therefore you are now free. Please believe it. To continually suffer the distressing effects of sin after adequate repentance, while not intended, is to deny the efficacy of the Savior's Atonement in your behalf."[8]

While not intended, when we do not allow ourselves to change and be forgiven, we are denying the Atonement by not trusting the Lord. In therapy, I often meet with people who are trying to forgive themselves and cannot, people who are anxious about their past mistakes. I meet with individuals who say they believe they have been forgiven, but they do not process the thought enough to truly trust in the Lord. The root of nonbelief is often anxiety.

A lot of individuals in this situation say something like this: "Well, you know, Sheldon, when I was sixteen . . ." and then they tell their story.

I will often ask, "Have you talked with your bishop about it?" The most common response is, "Oh yeah, many times." I respond, "Have there been times in your life when you have felt forgiven?" The most common response is, "There have been many occasions I have felt forgiven, but these feelings of guilt keep coming back."

I encourage them to believe Elder Scott and to process the thought that if we are stubbornly clinging to our guilt even after a bishop and stake president have cleared us and told us to move forward, we are denying the Atonement. If we continually deny the forgiveness process and tell ourselves there is still something more "I have to do," or "I need to confess one more time," then, as Elder Scott says, while not intended, we deny the Atonement. We deny its efficacy.

If we repeatedly process the sinful act, we begin to feel anxious. However, if someone can begin to process the times when they have felt forgiven and have felt the powerful effects of the Atonement, they will begin to feel more peace.

Let me give you another example to illustrate this point. I had a couple in my office one time who said, "Sheldon, we are in debt, big time, and we fight about it constantly. We know the prophets have said don't go into debt except for a modest home and maybe education and those kinds of things. Every single time someone talks about debt in general conference, we get really stressed and fight. What do we do?"

I asked them, "What direction are you headed? Are you going further into debt, or are you coming out?"

Do you see the difference in those two thoughts? If someone is thinking, "We are going further into debt, we do not have a plan, and this is financially ruining our marriage," their stress and anxiety will increase. If these thoughts are true, some anxiety is helpful. It's good to form a plan, to not go into debt, and to work together in a marriage.

However, if a couple is working on getting out of debt, they have a plan, and they have discussed the plan openly. Focusing on the plan and their forward direction will not lead to thoughts of anxiety. Direction is the key.

Therefore, when ruminating thoughts creep into our minds, we must ask ourselves, "What direction am I headed?" If you need a course correction, make it. If you are headed in a good direction, maintain it.

The Joseph Smith Translation of Psalm 30:5 reads, "For his anger kindleth against the wicked; they repent, and in a moment it is turned away, and they are in his favor, and he giveth them life." I love the phrase "in a moment it is turned away." The Lord wants us to continue forward, in the correct direction.

Another illustration of this thought process is when parents feel they could have done a better job with their children. I get a lot of parents who come in and say something like, "Sheldon, what do I do? My children are grown now, but they are not keeping the commandments. If I would have raised them differently, they probably would not be making these choices."

I often respond by suggesting that in the process of raising their children, they probably tried their best. I think that is true of most parents. They really do try their absolute best, and, of course, they can look back and say, "Oh, I know, but I wish I would have _____." I don't know a parent who cannot think of at least one thing they wish they would have done differently.

If a parent processes only their inadequacies, though, they are going to feel like a terrible parent. Most parents try to do their best, and if they process that thought, they will feel better. I look back at some of the things I've done as a parent and hope my children will forgive me. Even though I could certainly be more patient, I have tried my best from their birth and will continue to do so. I hope my children will know someday that I am trying my best.

If a parent begins to focus on all of the things they have done wrong, they are going to feel excessive worry, but if parents can process and refocus their thoughts on what direction they are headed, peace will often follow. Just because children are grown does not mean the parents have no influence. Parents with grown children can assist, be good grandparents, ask forgiveness, and be kind and full of praise for the good things their children do. Parenting can continue after the children have moved out. It is important to refocus your thoughts on the positive parenting you have done throughout your life.

ONE POSSIBLE CORRECT THOUGHT

Repentance is "a fresh view about God, about oneself, and about the world. . . . Repentance comes to mean a turning of the heart and will to God."[9] Worrying about the past will not change it and is a waste of emotional energy.

HELPFUL APPLICATION ACTIVITY

We often need to measure our goals to allow our minds to grab ahold of the direction we are headed. When doing this, it is helpful to choose one to two behaviors you are trying to improve. The more specific you are, the more helpful this activity will be. If you set a goal to "be a better parent," that goal is difficult to measure, but if you focus on a measurable goal that will lead to becoming a better parent, you can grow a great deal. For example, "I will read the scriptures with my children daily." We need to make sure these goals focus on becoming and not just doing, but we will discuss that concept in a later chapter.

Once you have chosen a behavior, state a goal and how you are going to measure this goal. Choose a reinforcement to encourage the completion of this goal. Remember to consistently ask yourself, "What direction am I headed?" Take these goals and put them somewhere you can see them.

Example:

Goal	Direction	Reinforcement
To pay an extra $250 toward our debt snowball each month.	Have we paid $250 this month, and are we planning to do so next month?	Every three months of paying the set amount to our debt snowball we will go to dinner at our favorite restaurant.

Principle 3 —

The Mark Is Christ, and if We Look Beyond Him, We Miss the Mark and Never Feel Whole Because We Cannot Be Whole without Him

SITUATION

Sally is on a quest to be righteous. She knows we are supposed to keep the commandments, and she has concluded that the way to become more like the Savior is to keep the rules. Every time she wants to improve, she makes a chart for the fridge and begins checking off scripture study, family home evening, and prayer. In a few weeks, she wants to be even more righteous, so she adds another item to the chart. Soon, checking off the chart and going through the motions is even more important than the benefit gained from doing the items on the chart.

Distorted Thought: Righteousness is achieved by following a series of checklists.

I have to be very careful whenever I use this example because I always get the look of death from the "chart keepers." It's that look that says, "Don't you dare say a word about my chart." So let me give a little disclaimer: now and then I have a chart on my fridge that I use with my children. I am not saying you should not use charts. What I'm trying to teach with hypothetical Sally is that, somehow, she believes the action of checking off the chart is just as important as the benefit of doing the action on the chart. I am referring to someone who believes that when Judgment Day arrives, we will need X amount of prayers, X amount of scripture study, and X amount of family home evenings, and if we hit those, we will be exalted—and if we don't, there's no hope.

I have seen this distorted belief about the gospel become debilitating to individuals. They set a strict regimen of rules, and as soon as they fall short, in their minds, all is lost. Some start to think, "The Church asks too much, and I can't keep up." The problem with this thought is not that the Church asks too much but that an individual detaches what they are to do from why they are to do it.

Jacob 4:14 gives us instruction and warning: "The Jews were a stiffnecked people; and they despised the words of plainness, and killed the prophets, and sought for things that they could not understand. Wherefore, because of their blindness, which blindness came by *looking beyond the mark*, they must needs fall" (emphasis added).

The first thing to consider is what or who the mark is portraying. The mark is the Savior. The aim in all we do in the Church should be Christ and His Atonement.

One year at youth conference, I was with my bishop and his two counselors, and they were teaching me how to shoot a bow and arrow, something I had never done before.

They got me all lined up and ready to go. I usually catch on to things quickly, so I thought I could get this figured out without a problem. I pulled the bow back and got ready to shoot. But they forgot to tell me that on this particular type of bow, there is an adjustable sight. So if you are forty yards away, you want to adjust the sight to that distance. If your sight is set to shoot from twenty yards away when you're standing forty yards away, you'll miss your mark, because while the arrow is traveling through the air, it starts to decline. You want your arrow arc to match your distance. That's the most scientific explanation I can come up with.

In this instance, I was about twenty yards away from the target, and I put the crosshair right on the bulls-eye and let it go. What I didn't realize until later was that I had lined up to shoot the arrow not twenty yards from where I stood but forty.

The arrow flew straight over the mark, and I think it was actually still gaining speed as it passed the target.

There are some people who don't even try in life. They are choosing to be rebellious and don't want to keep the commandments, but I don't think these are the people Jacob is talking about. I think he means those who are "religious" in their outward actions but who miss the point of the actions.

The Jews were a religious people, but they missed the mark. If we look up the word *Pharisees* in the Bible Dictionary, it says, "They prided themselves on their strict observance of the law, and on the care with which they avoided contact with things gentile. . . . They upheld the authority of oral tradition as of equal value with the written law."[10]

I do not think we need to spend time reviewing what the Lord said about the Pharisees or how He felt, but He definitely was not pleased with them. When we look at the Bible Dictionary definition, we realize that the Pharisees personally felt that they were a "religious people."

The Pharisees' battle cry was how strictly they could keep the law, but their main problem was that, over time, the law was not connected to its intended purpose. They kept the law, but they completely removed the Savior from it. They were doing what the law said and going through the motions, but they often did not know why they were keeping the law.

Think of the irony that these Pharisees, who had seen and performed animal sacrifice their whole lives, completely missed the fact that all of this symbolized and was designed to help them understand the Atonement. They missed the whole point.

In his book *Hearing the Voice of the Lord*, Elder Gerald N. Lund has a great quote about this concept. He says, "Obedience is not the same as righteousness. Jesus characterized their lives [meaning the Pharisees] with one word, 'Hypocrites!' They were motivated by a desire to be 'seen of men.'"[11]

The Pharisees were overly concerned with having their charts "checked off," and they became so consumed by the appearance of spirituality that they forgot the meaning behind their rituals and actions. The Lord said to the Pharisees and the scribes, "Woe unto you, scribes and Pharisees, hypocrites! for ye pay tithe of mint and anise and cummin, and have omitted the weightier matters of the law, judgment, mercy, and faith: these ought ye to have done, and not to leave the other undone" (Matthew 23:23). We learn that the Pharisees were paying tithing on herbs and spices but did not show mercy to fellow Jews. The Pharisees wanted to be able to check "tithing" off the list but ignored the most important commandments of loving God and loving their neighbor.

It was not just the Pharisees who had this challenge. King Noah and his priests also suffered from this blindness. Abinadi taught, "And now ye have said that salvation cometh by the law of Moses. I say unto you that it is expedient that ye should keep the law of Moses as yet; but I say unto you, that the time shall come when it shall no more be expedient to keep the law of Moses. And moreover, I say unto you, that salvation doth not come by the law alone; and were it not for the atonement, which God himself shall make for the sins and iniquities of his people, that they must unavoidably perish, notwithstanding the law of Moses" (Mosiah 13:27–28).

I want to share a classic example to help us connect this to anxiety. Assume someone wants to get rid of germs on their hands. What do they do? They wash their hands. Is there anything inappropriate about them washing their hands? No, not at all. Why? Because when they wash their hands, they get rid of germs, and that is important.

Hand washing can become a problem over time if someone begins to wash their hands excessively and it is no longer connected with getting rid of germs. I have clients come into the office who are trying to get rid of an excessive hand-washing habit, but many of these clients do not realize this is directly tied to anxiety. For these clients, washing hands has nothing to do with germs anymore. There are no germs on their hands— they are very, very clean. The reason people will continue washing their hands is that this ritualistic behavior lowers their anxiety about germs.

Let's say someone wants to become more like the Savior, and let's say that person decides they want to immerse themselves in the study of the scriptures as a means of coming closer to the Lord. There is nothing at all wrong with that. We need to immerse ourselves in the scriptures. But this would become a problem if over time we begin to check off studying the scriptures on a checklist and it has nothing to do with becoming like the Savior. All of a sudden, an individual reads the scriptures to mark off a chart, but they are not concerned about becoming more like the Son of God. When religious acts become disconnected from their intended outcome, we have cause to worry.

To illustrate this, I need to tell you a story, with my brother's permission. He once decided when he was in college that he was going to study the scriptures for a half hour a day, fifteen minutes in the Book of Mormon and fifteen minutes on a given topic. The topic he started with was charity.

So he opened up the scriptures, and he started studying. It had snowed about six inches the night before, and his roommate came into his room and asked, "Shad, I don't have a car, and work is a couple of miles away; could you give me a ride?" Shad said, "I can't; I'm right in the middle of something." Ironically, he returned to studying charity, and his roommate got ready to walk through the snow to work. Shad quickly realized what he had done, caught his roommate before he left, and took him to work. Shad is one of the most Christlike people I have ever met. Haven't we all found ourselves doing something similar?

When we start doing the things on our church list instead of living the gospel, it becomes disconnected from following the Savior, and it becomes very, very stressful. Suddenly, church feels like a routine, it feels like we are not growing or progressing, and we worry a lot. Many times, we go through the motions and miss the whole point. How many of you, like me, have been guilty of yelling at the kids to get them gathered for family prayer? How many of you, like me, have ever served for the wrong reason, whether it was to be seen or to get praise or to make your church reputation look really shiny? How many of you, like me, have not really communicated with Heavenly Father through prayer, but you've prayed because that is what we are "supposed to do"? How many of you, like me, have read the scriptures to check them off the list but have lost the true meaning of scripture study?

One morning I had an experience in which the Lord taught me a great truth. I know that it may seem simple, but it touched my heart.

I had set a goal to study my scriptures in the morning. I got up that particular morning to begin scripture study, and I had about forty-five minutes. I was really excited. I studied for about fifteen minutes, and it was great because it was early enough that no one was awake. Our five little kids, who are usually bouncing off the walls, were still quiet. It was just my time.

I looked over and saw the sink full of dishes from the night before. I thought I heard the Lord whisper to me, "Why don't you stop studying your scriptures and go clean the dishes?"

Some might ask, "Why would the Lord tell you to stop studying the scriptures?" So at first glance, it may seem like I had not received revelation. I'm not implying that we should not study our scriptures—please do not misunderstand me—but I think what I learned in that moment was, while I was studying my scriptures to try to learn how to become like the Savior, through the power of the Holy Ghost, He told me what He might do if He were in my place. He would probably serve when He had a chance to serve.

Elder Lynn G. Robbins once said,

> In helping children discover who they are and helping strengthen their self-worth, we can appropriately compliment their achievement or behavior—the *do*. But it would be even wiser to focus our primary praise on their character and beliefs—who they *are*.
>
> In a game of sports, a wise way to compliment our children's performance—*do*—would be through the point of view of *be*—like their energy, perseverance, poise in the

face of adversity, etc.—thus complimenting both *be* and *do*.[12]

If our focus centers on the "be" and not just the "do," we will begin to live the gospel the way the Lord intends us to live it. He wants us to become something, not just do something.

I truly believe that we need to act for the right reasons. For example, if we fast with no reason in mind, it is more difficult. In my case, if I fast without a real purpose, I find excuses to eat. But if I have a reason for fasting, it's harder for me to justify eating and breaking that specific commitment. I think we can use that analogy in every principle of the gospel: When we attend sacrament meeting, we should think deeply about the Savior and His Atonement; when we are reading our scriptures, we should study with real intent, looking for principles that will help us become like the Savior and resolving to become more like Him in all we do and say.

I meet with a lot of clients who are burned out; they are tired and don't want to continue doing what they've been doing. Most of the time, they are wonderful, wonderful people, but they are moving at an incredible pace and doing so for the wrong reasons. They have forgotten that religious acts are to help us become like and draw us closer to our Father.

One Possible Correct Thought

Being righteous and doing good is more important than the appearance of being righteous and doing good. The reason we do anything in the gospel is to become more like the Savior.

It is more important that I read the scriptures with the intent to become like the Savior than to read the scriptures with the intent to say I did it. It is more important to fast for a reason and to grow closer to the Lord than to fast because that is what we are supposed to do on the first Sunday. It is more important for me to go home teaching and to honestly and sincerely be concerned about my families and their needs than to report at the end of the month that, "Yep, I did it."

I truly believe that we need to be able to report at the end of the month that we did it, but I think if that is our *only* goal, if we only go through the motions, after awhile we start to worry too much about going through the motions and not enough about the true intent of home teaching or any other gospel action.

Our goal should not only include doing what is right, but it should also include *being* what is right. Remember that the Lord knows all and sees all, and it really only matters what He thinks.

HELPFUL APPLICATION ACTIVITY

If we want to get to the root of our actions, it is often helpful to do an activity called the "Why" game. The "Why" game requires a lot of honesty, so it is best done alone, using a journal.

The point of the activity is to figure out the reasons we are doing a certain activity and also to identify what we want our real motives to be. A good way to get to this outcome is to continually ask yourself "why" until you get closer to the root.

For example, if someone felt that they needed to study the scriptures more often than they currently are, they might follow a pattern similar to this:

I need to study the scriptures. Why?

Because I know it will bless my life. Why?

Because the prophet has taught that we will come closer to the Lord. Why?

Because we can read about the Savior's life and feel the Spirit. Why?

Because when I read about the Savior, it invites the Spirit so I can know how to become like Him. Why?

In order to become more like the Savior and to feel the Spirit, I will study the word of God to learn how to act each day.

This final reason can help you find better motivation than simply stating, "I need to study the scriptures." This process takes honesty and determination to stick with it. Taking time to truly ponder why you are really doing what you are doing can be beneficial for anyone. This process should be done multiple times in order to make a change.

Principle 4 —

Learn to Find Joy in the Journey

SITUATION

I will be happy when _____. Fill in the blank: When I go on a mission. When I get off a mission. When I get married. When I finish school. When I have children. When the children are in school. When the children move out. When I'm out of debt. When I have grandchildren. When I retire. When I go on another mission. Or, when I die.

Doctrine and Covenants 138:50 says, "For the dead had looked upon the long absence of their spirits from their bodies as a bondage."

One day when I was reading this, the thought came into my mind, *Even in the spirit world, it's possible to say, "I'll be happy when _____." "I'll be happy when I'm resurrected."*

This process never stops. It has the possibility of going on for a very long time.

Distorted Thought: When all my hopes and dreams are realized, then I'll feel happy.

What is wrong with this thought process? We will always have more hopes and dreams than we can realize. In fact, I cannot think of a time in my life when I have not thought, *I will be happy at the next stage.* It seems as though we often live life thinking that the next stop is happiness, and when we get there, we realize that happiness is still one more stop away. We must learn that happiness can be achieved at each stage in life and not at some distant point in the future.

President Thomas S. Monson said, "This is our one and only chance at mortal life—here and now. The longer we live, the greater is our realization that it is brief. Opportunities come, and then they are gone. I believe that among *the greatest lessons* we are to learn in this short sojourn upon the earth are lessons that help us distinguish between what is important and what is not. I plead with you to not let those most important things pass you by as you plan for that illusive and nonexistent future when you will have time to do all that you want to do. Instead, find joy in the journey—now."[13]

I want to point out that when a prophet speaks, we should always listen, and we should pay extra attention when prophets use words such as *greatest lessons*. What a wonderful thought, that we need to find joy in this day and not put our joy off for some time in the future.

I think everyone does this to some extent. In Helaman 7, great things are about to happen to Nephi and his people. Nephi will soon receive the sealing power and be "empowered to bind and loose on earth and in heaven" (Helaman 10, chapter heading). Look at how he describes Nephi and Lehi of old in Helaman 7:7: "Oh, that I could have had my days in the days when my father Nephi first came out of the land of Jerusalem, that I could have joyed with him in the promised land; then were his people easy to be entreated, firm to keep the commandments of God, and slow to be led to do iniquity; and they were quick to hearken unto the words of the Lord."

Nephi had to be speaking of specific situations because there is definite evidence that the earlier Nephite people were *not* always easy to be entreated, and there were times when they were certainly *not* keeping the commandments. For instance, if we talk about the story of Laman and Lemuel, we could find examples that they were not exactly "easy to be entreated in keeping the commandments."

Laman and Lemuel murmured most of the time, they had a hard time trusting the Lord, and they struggled to keep the commandments; in fact, the only time Laman and Lemuel did not murmur was when they were asked to return to Jerusalem to find Ishmael and his daughters—that is the one and only time they were strictly obedient in the scriptures. And still, Nephi wishes he could go back to those days when men were easy to be entreated.

We must be certain that we recognize that there are great and wonderful events in our current life situation. It's easy to say, "If I could only have lived in the days of Nephi to watch him receive the power to seal in heaven and earth," or "I wish I lived in the times of Joseph Smith, when the Saints were easy to be entreated." That's true to a point, but while there were some Saints who were easy to be entreated, there were certainly others who weren't. It's true in every stage of history. We have a tendency to glorify the past the same way we do the future. See history for what it was, both good and bad, and learn to see your own life for what it truly is, both good and bad. It's easy to glorify the past or the unknown future. Sometimes we focus too much on the current trials we are coping with because they are happening to us today. If we do this too much, it keeps us from appreciating the good in every day. Learn to appreciate the phase that you are in.

My small family leads a busy life. We go through an endless cycle of laundry, dishes, cleaning, homework, runny noses, and diapers. I want to share a few stories about my children that have helped me understand the joy in my current journey.

My son McKay plays tackle football. When he was in the second grade, he played his first year. If you have never seen second-grade tackle football, it's like herding cats. In fact, McKay came up to me halfway through the season and said, "Hey, Dad, am I on offense or defense right now?" He had already run about twelve plays, and I thought, this is a major concern. He's played half the game, and he doesn't know if he's on offense or defense.

One day, he lined up in practice to do his tackling drill, and he went up against this boy in practice who was a giant of a second grader. This other boy was old for his grade and huge for his age. McKay, on the other hand, was young for his grade and small for his age. McKay lined up head-to-head and got run through; I mean, the other boy didn't even slow down. He hit McKay hard, and I remember thinking, *I hope he's not injured too badly.* The coach called for a water break, and McKay hopped up and ran over to me. He gave me a thumbs up and said, "Dad, did you see how fast I got up when that boy hit me?" I laughed and thought, *I have got to remember this and write it in my journal because when he's sixteen, I'll miss this type of response.*

I have another son named Kimball. We once had a Primary presentation in which Kimball participated. One day, he came up to my wife and me, crying, and said, "Mom, Dad, I don't want to do my part." He was very upset. We told him, "You don't have to do your part if you don't want to." We were not going to force him, but his reluctant attitude surprised us because normally he wasn't that shy. Kimball's part was to stand and say the line, "I am a child of God." The day of the practice, the Sunday before the Primary presentation, Kimball went up to the pulpit, and it looked like he had decided to say it after all. He grabbed the microphone and began to sing, "I Am a Child of God"—sing, not say. Kimball thought that his part in the program was to sing a solo. No wonder he was nervous. But he did it anyway. I will not get that priceless experience back when he is a teenager.

One day my third son, Joseph, was sitting at the table drinking out of a straw. He paused, looked up at me with a smile, and said, "Dad, look, the straw works backwards." He flipped the straw over and started to suck out of the bottom, and sure enough, it did. Nicole and I laughed about that for a long time.

Having little kids at home is difficult, and we can choose to focus on the endless dishes, diapers, laundry, and noise, or we can remember these experiences we will never get back, and they will help us focus on the good things and not just the hard things of the current stage.

Sometimes it feels like the phase we're in is never going to end. President Thomas S. Monson spoke of that when he said,

> If you are still in the process of raising children, be aware that the tiny fingerprints that show up on almost every newly cleaned surface, the toys scattered about the house, the piles and piles of laundry to be tackled will disappear all too soon. And that you will—to your surprise—miss them profoundly.
>
> Stresses come in our life regardless of our circumstances. We must deal with them the best we can, but we should not let them get in the way of what is most important. *And what is most important, almost always, involves the people around us.*[14]

I have asked hundreds of grandparents if they miss having their small children at home. The overwhelming response is yes, they miss this stage a lot. I have also asked hundreds of parents who still have small children at home if they are excited for the "grandparent stage." As you would probably guess, these parents are eager for that time to come. It sounds like a breeze after what they go through every day. Isn't it ironic how these two groups envy the other's stage? We would all do well to learn how to love our current stage.

President Dieter F. Uchtdorf said, "If life and its rushed pace and many stresses have made it difficult for you to feel like rejoicing, then perhaps now is a good time to refocus on what *matters most*."[15]

One day we are going to profoundly miss the experiences of the past. One day our current situation will be our past, and it will be these precious days we miss. The day will come when all we want is second grade football, Primary programs, and backward straws, but the day will also come when we will miss the teenage years, the mission field, the newlywed stage, or the young children at home. Appreciate the moment you are in.

Elder Richard G. Scott told a story in conference that inspired me. He said,

> Once I learned an important lesson from my wife. I traveled extensively in my profession. I had been gone almost two weeks and returned home one Saturday morning. I had four hours before I needed to attend another meeting. I noticed that our little washing machine had broken down and my wife was washing the clothes by hand. I began to fix the machine.
>
> Jeanene came by and said, "Rich, what are you doing?"
>
> I said, "I'm repairing the washing machine so you don't have to do this by hand."
>
> She said, "No. Go play with the children."
>
> I said, "I can play with the children anytime. I want to help you."
>
> Then she said, "Richard, please go play with the children."
>
> When she spoke to me that authoritatively, I obeyed.
>
> I had a marvelous time with our children. We chased each other around and rolled in the fall leaves. Later I went to my meeting. I probably would have forgotten that experience were it not for the lesson that she wanted me to learn.[16]

This story is a wonderful example that reminds us to make what is most important our priority. These moments do not happen by accident. We must make an effort to recognize and focus on what matters most.

ONE POSSIBLE CORRECT THOUGHT

I will someday miss today, so I must make the most of it now.

When we begin to process the thought that "happiness is just around the corner," we should confront and change that thought. When we process the thought over and over again that we must make the most of today because there is something we will miss about it in the future, we feel encouraged. When someone realizes they are going to miss something about today, it lowers their anxiety about that elusive future President Monson refers to.

Helpful Application Activity

In order to train your brain to think about what matters most, make this a topic in your journal. Try asking yourself the question, "What will I miss about today?" Then write about this question.

When we do this, we start to recognize that there are experiences today that we will one day miss, and we begin to live with appreciation for those precious moments. If I find myself forgetting the importance of every single day, I begin keeping my journal this way, and I am able to relish and focus on the small, wonderful gifts unique to each day.

Principle 5 –

Becoming More Righteous Does Not Guarantee Others Will Like Us

We know doctrinally that it cannot be correct to think that if we become more righteous, people will like us. The best example to illustrate this point is our Lord and Savior Himself. He was perfect, and people still hated Him. It is important to realize that others not liking the Savior was not the Savior's fault.

In fact, one time I had a lady in my office who said, "Sheldon, I just can't do it anymore. People don't like me, and I know it's because I'm messing up."

I started to lead her on. "So you feel if you became better and better, then more and more people would like you."

"Yes, that's right."

I finally got her going a little bit more, and then I said, "Like the Savior." She looked at me as if I had just rocked her entire mental foundation and said, "What do you mean?"

"Well, He was perfect," I said. "He never sinned, so everyone must have loved Him."

She recognized quickly that becoming better did not guarantee social acceptance.

SITUATION

John has served his heart out in his ward. He goes to Scout camp every year, helps people move all the time, and signs up to clean the building. He smiles at others in the ward and tries to reach out, but no matter how hard he tries, he feels someone in the ward is always mad at him. He worries because he wants to be loving and kind to others and wonders what he is doing wrong to cause others to not like him.

Distorted Thought: If I become a better person, people will like and appreciate me.

We should be kind and loving as Latter-day Saints. We should appreciate and respect others. Notice that this principle only focuses on what we can do. We do not have control over what others think.

Elder David A. Bednar made this point in a talk he gave in general conference. He said,

> Understanding that the church is a learning laboratory helps us to prepare for an inevitable reality. In some way and at some time, someone in this Church will do or say something that could be considered offensive. Such an event will surely happen to each and every one of us—and it certainly will occur more than once. Though people may not intend to injure or offend us, they nonetheless can be inconsiderate and tactless.
>
> You and I cannot control the intentions or behavior of other people. However, we do determine how we will act. Please remember that you and I are agents endowed with moral agency, and we can choose not to be offended.[17]

I love this quote by Elder Bednar. He's pointing out that the situation or opportunity for offense, if it has not already occurred, *will* occur. Someone will be rude, tactless, or inconsiderate. He also suggests this situation will occur more than once.

The Lord says in Matthew 22:39, "Thou shalt love thy neighbor as thyself." I want you to notice something about this verse. It is implying and assuming that we appreciate and respect ourselves. Look at the verse again. "Thou shalt love thy neighbour as *thyself*." I have met people who would not have very many friends if they treated others like they treat themselves.

Why are people so hard on themselves? Why do people automatically assume that if someone does not like them, it is because of something they did wrong? These are difficult questions to answer. I do not know of anyone who wants someone not to like them. But unfortunately, because we are all imperfect mortals, we are going to bump into each other in rude and inconsiderate ways.

There are times in the Church when someone will do something to us that could be taken as offensive. It does not mean we did anything wrong. It also does not mean they do not like us.

Regrettably, though, it could be that someone does not like us. I do not bring this up to be negative. I have met with many clients in my office who have expressed these feelings and thoughts. As soon as someone gives them negative feedback, they internalize it, personalize it, and often become defined by it. If you truly feel that someone doesn't like you, do the best you can to be polite and kind, but outside of that, you don't have control.

Let me use an example to illustrate this. If you remember in the later part of the Book of Mormon, Mormon is a warrior, leader of the Nephites, and prophet.

In Mormon 2:23, pay attention to who Mormon is quoting. He urges his people to "fight for their wives, and their children, and their houses, and their homes."

It sounds a lot like Captain Moroni. We know that Mormon loved and honored Captain Moroni from Mormon's comments about the captain: "If all men had been, and were, and ever would be, like unto Moroni, behold, the very powers of hell would have been shaken forever" (Alma 48:17). Later, Mormon even names his own son Moroni. It might make sense that Mormon would quote from his hero to rally the Nephites in a great time of need.

What happened when Captain Moroni gave his talk? People rent their clothes and threw them at his feet, making covenants. The people loved him; they rallied, they fought, and they were great warriors. They won the war.

Look what happens when Mormon gives a similar speech: "My words did arouse them *somewhat* to vigor, insomuch that they did not *flee from before the Lamanites*" (Mormon 2:24; emphasis added). Mormon is saying, "Well, I guess we didn't run from them. I guess that's the best I can say for us right now—when we went to war, we didn't retreat. That's all I got."

Yes, later in the chapter, the Nephites rally and win the battle, but we learn an important lesson from this story. Do you see how Mormon could have walked away and said to himself, "What is wrong with me? When Captain Moroni gave that speech, his troops rallied and fought with honor." In this example, the Nephites' reaction is not Mormon's problem. It's the Nephites' problem. Mormon was not doing anything wrong. The Nephites at this time were becoming wicked, and they were not following their prophet and leader.

In every situation in life, others will always be able to interpret and feel how they want to feel. Just as Mormon did not have control over how the Nephites would react to his message, we do not have control over how someone reacts to us. Sometimes people are offended; they choose to be offended by something we do. It does not mean we did something wrong. It might mean *they* are making poor choices. I would love to tell you that all people have pure motives and intentions; however, unfortunately, sometimes people are rude and will not like us no matter how hard we try. In these situations, we need to realize it is not our responsibility to carry the emotional weight of someone else's poor choices.

Elder Quentin L. Cook, speaking of the women of the Church, said,

> Our sisters throughout the Church consistently "succor the weak, lift up the hands which hang down, and strengthen the feeble knees."
>
> One Relief Society president who acknowledged this extraordinary service said, "Even when the sisters serve, they are thinking, '*If only I could have done more!*' *Though they are not perfect and all face individual struggles*, their faith in a loving Father in Heaven and the assurance of the atoning sacrifice of the Savior permeates their lives.[18]

Members of this great Church—individuals who are truly remarkable— are constantly asking themselves, "What could I have done more?" If this is your natural inclination, then it may be difficult to ever feel you have done "enough." May I emphasize that even when you do all you can and serve others, often without recognition, there will, unfortunately, still be people who will not appreciate and acknowledge your hard work. But do not stop doing great deeds.

Many of the individuals with whom I counsel are constant "people pleasers." It is not wrong to want others to like us, but if our actions continue to change in order to have others like us, we will be anxious, and our actions will always depend on what "the group" wants.

I am so grateful that the Savior cared more about what Father thought than what the Pharisees thought. I am so grateful that Joseph Smith cared more about what the Lord thought than what Governor Ford thought, and I am so grateful that our dear modern prophets care more about what the Lord thinks than what the evening news thinks. Likewise, we must focus on caring more about what the Lord thinks than what neighbors, ward members, and even friends think.

One Possible Correct Thought

I should be as Christlike as I can. I will determine to fear God more than man and be less concerned with what others think of me because I cannot control what they think.

Do you see the two parts there? Part one: we do need to be as kind, loving, and Christlike as we can be, but at that point, we need to leave it up to others to make their own choices.

There may be times when people choose to be offended by what we say or do, but what we need to focus on is being more concerned with what Heavenly Father thinks of us rather than what other people think of us.

Let me give you a few examples to illustrate this point. When someone starts to feel a little nervous about every interaction they have with others, they will often try to overcompensate and do anything to gain approval. Carmen feels that her boss is disapproving of things she is doing at work, so she automatically internalizes it by saying, "I'm not a good employee," or "I'm doing something wrong." She tries to gain approval somehow, and she starts to overcompensate. She often approaches her boss and asks random questions to try to gain some positive feedback, which the boss does not give. Carmen wonders again, "What did I do wrong?" Carmen then sends an e-mail expressing her concern and hoping the boss will respond with an outpouring of encouragement. Instead, the boss responds with a short, to-the-point response. Carmen reads too much into the response and feels she is now digging herself a hole. She sets up a special appointment to do more to gain the boss's approval. At this point, Carmen is becoming high maintenance, and the boss is getting annoyed. Carmen continues to seek positive feedback, but the harder she tries, the more resistance the boss gives because he now finds Carmen annoying.

I have heard this type of experience dozens of times. My advice would be to relax, do what you can, and worry less what others think. Remember that you cannot control anyone else's emotions, and often, the harder you try, the more you may annoy.

We need to be as Christlike as we can, but remember that others have their agency, and they may not be kind to us. If someone is not kind to us, that does not automatically mean that we are the problem.

HELPFUL APPLICATION ACTIVITY

If you find yourself worrying too much what others think, then identify how much control you have and what you can do with that control. For example, if I worry that someone in my ward does not like me, I can sit down and ask myself the question, "How much control do I have?"

When you ask yourself this question, there are two ends of the spectrum—total control and no control. Very few, if any, situations will fall into one of these categories in the spectrum. Usually, situations fall somewhere in between.

The first thing you can do is decide what you have control of and what you do not. If someone does not like you, you can control how kind, polite, and respectful you are. You can control the amount of time you think about it, and you can control your ability to forgive. You cannot control whether the person will be polite in return, and you cannot control if the person will talk about you to their neighbors or other ward members. Worrying about it will not increase or decrease the odds of someone else changing their opinion about you.

Principle 6 –
We Have Limited Information,
So We Should Avoid Seeing the Future Negatively

SITUATION

John has a bad habit of "connecting the dots" in his head, and when he does this, it's often in a negative pattern. In his mind, he says, "The washer broke, and we have no money, so we had to buy another one using the credit card because we have nothing in savings. We have two thousand dollars on the credit card now, and we can't pay it off. We can't help our oldest with college tuition this semester, and I don't know what she's going to do. I'll probably need a second job—I don't know when I'm going to have the time to do that. If I get a second job, it's going to take me away from the kids, and then we're going to have a hard time having family prayer and scripture study. And if we can't do that, I don't know what's going to happen to them. . . ."

Do you see what John is doing? The washer broke, and he's already connected the dots so that his children are going to be eternally scarred. This connection happened quickly in his mind. The brain processes very, very quickly. We often do this—negatively connect the dots so fast that we don't even realize we're doing it—until it's too late and we've created unnecessary anxiety in our lives.

Distorted Thought: This single event is enough evidence to draw a general conclusion about myself or the future.

Think of a current challenge in your life, a difficult trial, or something you're struggling with right now, and negatively connect the dots. It's actually kind of fun. Think of as many specific steps as you can and plan it all the way out to the worst-case scenario. Be as specific as you can, like John was after his washer broke.

Now, take the same exact event and do a positive connection of the dots. Think of as many steps as you can and end with the best-case scenario.

When you're done, look at the first step of the negative pattern and the first step of the positive pattern. Finally, decide what you can do to increase the odds that your next step is in the positive direction.

John connected the dots all the way down to an event years away that he was "sure" was going to happen. If we flip the situation around, there are definitely other possibilities. Maybe if he were to slow down and think through the positive options, he would realize, "Oh, wait, I get a tax return in two weeks. I'll pay off the credit card, and everything will be fine."

I'm using John and his washing machine as a simplistic example, but when things go wrong in our lives, there can be a positive connection of the dots that is just as likely and, in fact, more likely to occur than a purely negative chain reaction.

Let's look at an example in 1 Nephi 16:35; look at the negative connection the daughters of Ishmael start to make: "And it came to pass that the daughters of Ishmael did mourn exceedingly, because of the loss of their father." Okay so far; their reaction is understandable. They've lost their father, they are mourning, and they are having a difficult time. The verse continues: ". . . because of their afflictions in the wilderness; and they did murmur against my father, because he had brought them out of the land of Jerusalem, saying: Our father is dead; yea, and we have wandered much in the wilderness, and we have suffered much affliction, hunger, thirst, and fatigue; and after all these sufferings *we must perish* in the wilderness with hunger" (emphasis added).

In the daughters' minds, death is the only outcome. After everything else, we are all going to starve to death. The most ironic part about this entire statement is that they do not die, they do not starve to death, and they do not perish. None of these things actually happens. Well, their father does die, they do have affliction, they have hunger, they have thirst, and they have fatigue. These things actually do happen to them, but the end is far different from their connect-the-dots conclusion.

Later in the chapter, Nephi does a miraculous job of positively connecting the dots. Listen to what he says in verse 39: "And it came to pass that the Lord was with us, yea, even the voice of the Lord came and did speak many words unto them, and did chasten them exceedingly; and after they were chastened by the voice of the Lord they did turn away their anger, and did repent of their sins, insomuch that the *Lord did bless us again with food, that we did not perish*" (emphasis added).

Take note that he added, "We did not perish."

Let's look at Nephi's connections. He said, "The Lord was with us." Nephi was there. He experienced similar events to the daughters of Ishmael. It is important to remember that our events do not govern our emotions. We have all seen individuals who have experienced extremely difficult situations and responded quite well. On the other hand, we have seen individuals experience relatively routine challenges and become extremely depressed.

People often come to therapy because they have experienced a negative event. We all have those bad days. President Boyd K. Packer has said,

> To suffer some anxiety, some depression, some disappointment, even some failure is normal.
>
> Teach our members that if they have a good, miserable day once in a while, or several in a row, to stand steady and face them. Things will straighten out.
>
> There is great purpose in our struggle in life.[19]

Sometimes I get discouraged when people forget this is the case. We should expect to have bad days—it is part of mortality. Not realizing this can become a problem when someone starts to draw general conclusions about the future because of a single negative event. It's dangerous because we don't have enough evidence to know what is going to happen.

I will often ask clients, "How have you coped with this in the past?" Usually, I find out that the person has already dealt with a similar situation in their life. In fact, I believe that this is one of the main reasons we keep journals and study the scriptures—so people can look back and recognize how they've successfully passed through hard things before.

When we keep a journal, we write about challenges and problems, but maybe more importantly, we write about how the Lord has helped us through certain situations. When we study the scriptures, we are able to read about the challenges and problems of the prophets of old, how they turned to the Lord, and how the Lord blessed them.

I had an individual in therapy one time who'd lost his job. He was in my office, not because he had lost his job but because he felt his unemployment status completely defined him as a human being. He felt that he was worth nothing, that he was not a good father or husband, and that he was not well enough educated nor had enough training. These thoughts would continue until his feelings would spiral downward. I thought, *How in the world can you draw all of these conclusions because your company shut down?* It wasn't his fault the company closed, yet he had found all of these reasons for why he was no good. This man took one piece of evidence and used it to draw negative conclusions about himself.

As members of the Church, we have so many reasons to be optimistic about the future. Elder Neil L. Andersen said, "Those awaiting the Savior's coming will 'look for [Him].' And He has promised, 'I will come'! The righteous will see Him 'in the clouds of heaven [with all the holy angels], clothed with power and great glory.' 'An angel shall sound his trump, and the saints . . . from the four quarters of the earth' will 'be caught up to meet him.' Those 'that have slept,' meaning those worthy Saints who have died, 'shall [also] come forth to meet [Him].'"[20]

We know that the King of Kings will return one day. Yes, there will be challenges in mortality. Yes, we will have trials in this mortal sojourn. Yes, we will experience the negative effects of others' agency. However, one day, the King of Kings, our Lord and Master, our Redeemer and Savior, will return to rule planet Earth, and because of that, we can have faith and optimism about what lies ahead.

The Lord will allow us to struggle and will try us often in mortality. I love the story of Hagar in the Old Testament. Hagar and her son are "cast out of Abraham's household" (Genesis 21, chapter heading). Hagar must feel alone, forgotten, and powerless. She hits a point when her water is gone and she is certain her son is going to die. She places Ishmael under a shrub and walks away, probably so she does not have to see him die.

Hagar sits down and pours out her heart. Genesis 21:17 says, "And God heard the voice of the lad; and the angel of God called to Hagar out of heaven, and said unto her, What aileth thee Hagar?" If we were to rephrase the question in contemporary language, we would say, "What's wrong?" or "What's the matter?"

In this moment of ultimate, desperate despair, "God opened her eyes, and she saw a well of water" (Genesis 21:19).

Sometimes the Lord allows us to struggle until the last moment before He shows us where the well of water is. This increases the odds that we'll recognize the Lord's hand and see that *He* has opened our eyes.

As with Hagar, sometimes our experiences in the desert lead to an oasis. We need to have faith that one negative event is not enough to draw a general conclusion about the entire future because the Lord can and will (if we are willing) provide a way for us to overcome the moment's trial.

It is important to remember that one event in life does not govern how the rest of the events will turn out. If we can slow down and realize that the current situation is just one situation, we will be more likely to move through a negative event with confidence. Sometimes our perceived negative events turn out to be our moments of greatest growth.

ONE POSSIBLE CORRECT THOUGHT

This single piece of evidence is not enough information to draw general conclusions about the future. There are multiple possible, outcomes, and I must do my best to pursue the best one.

It is important to understand that we cannot know the final result from one piece of information. A single event is exactly that—single. Events in life *are* interconnected, but we must learn to not draw general negative conclusions from just one piece of evidence.

HELPFUL APPLICATION ACTIVITY

Think about a situation in your life that is particularly challenging. Write out some of the thoughts you process when you feel stressed. Try to be as specific as possible. When you have detailed these steps in a nonthreatening environment, you will see this distorted process more clearly.

Now write other possible solutions or outcomes to this situation. When you are looking at both scenarios, identify what you can do to increase the odds of bringing about the positive outcome. When you do this in a quiet setting, it will help when the pressure is on. When you get stressed, your mind often goes immediately to the worst-case scenario. If you have spent time processing other outcomes, your mind has real experiences to grab on to.

Principle 7 —
By Grace We Are Saved

SITUATION

Peter is an Eagle Scout, and he was assistant to the president on his mission. He home teaches every month, pays an honest tithe, diligently serves in his callings, has seven years of food storage, has traced his family history back as far as records exist, has family home evening every Monday, has never missed a day of scripture study, sings in the choir, and is pleasant and kind to his wife—and Peter is stressed because he still feels inadequate.

> *Distorted Thought: I can somehow merit exaltation because of my own best efforts.*

Where is the distortion in this?

Some feel that they must—on their effort alone—merit exaltation, when the absolute truth is that no matter how good any of us is, we are just not going to make it without the Savior.

In the Bible Dictionary, the definition of *grace* states, "It is likewise through the grace of the Lord that individuals, through faith in the atonement of Jesus Christ and repentance of their sins, *receive strength and assistance to do good works*. That they otherwise would not be able to maintain if left to their own means. This grace is an enabling power that allows men and women to lay hold on eternal life and exaltation after they have *expended their own best efforts*."[21]

Notice the first part of that definition: the grace of our Savior allows us to do the good things we can do in life. In other words, after we have done all that we can do, we still need the grace of the Savior in order to be saved.

Many members of the Church forget that no matter how good they become, without the Atonement of Christ, they are lost.

Elder Russell M. Nelson has said,

> Let us do the best we can and try to improve each day. When our imperfections appear, we can keep trying to correct them. We can be more forgiving of flaws in ourselves and among those we love. We can be comforted and forbearing. The Lord taught, 'Ye are not able to abide the presence of God now . . . ; wherefore, continue in patience until ye are perfected.
>
> We need not be dismayed if our earnest efforts toward perfection now seem so arduous and endless. *Perfection is pending. It can come in full only after the Resurrection and only through the Lord.*22

I want to point out two things Elder Nelson says. One, he says perfection can come in full only *after* the Resurrection, and two, it can come only through the Lord. If we feel we are going to obtain perfection on our own merits, we will always come up short. We will never reach that goal.

In fact, in 2 Nephi 9, Jacob is very, very clear on this subject. Look at verses 8–9: "For behold, if the flesh should rise no more our spirits must become subject to that angel who fell from before the presence of the Eternal God, and became the devil, to rise no more. And our spirits must have become like unto him"—and notice this part—"and we become devils, angels to a devil."

Jacob points out that *without the Atonement of Jesus Christ*, it doesn't matter how much we try, how many things we do that are wonderful in this life, we have no hope. To help us identify the importance and the need of the Atonement in our lives, President Ezra Taft Benson said, "Just as man does not really desire food until he is hungry, so he does not desire salvation of Christ until he knows why he needs Christ."23

I really like the analogy of using food to help us understand our need for the Atonement. I love Thanksgiving—it's probably my favorite holiday of the year. When I was a kid, my mother cooked wonderful Thanksgiving dinners, and now my wife does. I always eat a little bit of everything so I'm sure to not miss anything. I love the pie, the turkey, the stuffing, and the mashed potatoes. I love everything. So here's the question: an hour after Thanksgiving dinner, how often do we think of eating more food? If you eat like I do, then one hour later, you're still pretty full, which means you're not thinking about eating food at all. In fact, the thought of it probably makes you a little nauseated. I personally don't want it. I don't need it—until about three hours later, and then I really want turkey sandwiches. But up until that point, I don't have any use for food because I'm still so full.

Contrast the feeling of being full with the feeling of hunger. I've attended Scout camp for about seven years in a row with the boys in my ward. The food has usually been really good, and there have been great dutch oven dinners—but that is not always the case.

Those of you who have dealt with Scouts know that one of the things they try to do during camp is earn the cooking merit badge. It's a true act of faith on the part of the leaders who attend to turn a meal over to the twelve-year-old boys to cook and then actually come together and eat it when they are done doing whatever it is they do to it. By the time the meal is done and ready to serve, we look at it and think, *There is not a chance in the world I'm going to eat that.*

A week at Scout camp is a much better way to lose five to ten pounds than many of the great diet programs I've seen advertised. I lose about five pounds every single time I go. And I never thought Tang could become a dessert, but at Scout camp, it can. It's the only thing with flavor by the end of the week.

So ask me when I get home from camp how much I want good food. I've thought about it constantly, all week, and I want it badly by the time camp ends. I believe this is what President Benson meant. We do not desire the Savior until we understand why we need Him. Only then will we have a greater desire for His Atonement.

In this analogy, we need to understand that we are all in the Scout camp category. There is not one of us who can be made "full" without the Atonement. We are absolutely, every single one of us, lost without Him. But with Him, we do have hope to gain everlasting life. He is the way. No matter how hard we try, we will always fall into the Scout camp category. We're always going to be hungry, and we need Him to fill us. When we understand this concept, our attention shifts from *our inability* to *His ability* to save.

Realizing that we are imperfect should not push us away from the Savior but draw us near to Him. One day I asked a young man who was extremely hard on himself if he thought he would go to the celestial kingdom if he were to die that day. He responded that there was no way he was going to the celestial kingdom. I asked him why, and he started to tell me all the things he had done wrong. I knew this young man well enough to know that he was worthy of a temple recommend and that he attended often.

I finally got to the question I wanted to ask: "If the Lord is not going to save you, who is He going to save?"

"What do you mean?" he asked.

"Well," I said, "His plan is the plan of salvation, not the plan of damnation. So I'm just wondering, who do you think the Savior is going to save if He doesn't save faithful Latter-day Saints who attend the temple?"

I knew of a woman in her eighties who was the most faithful sister I have possibly ever met. One day she expressed her inability to ever feel good enough in the Church. This sister had served multiple missions with her husband and had served in the temple almost daily. Again, the question came to my mind, "If the Lord does not save her, who is He going to save?"

I do not want to be misunderstood. I am in no way pretending that I can tell people they are going to be saved. Our lives are works in progress, but we should have some level of confidence that the Lord is trying to save us and not damn us. Hopefully our weaknesses and shortcomings lead us to the Savior and not away from Him. Hopefully His goodness and willingness to forgive and save increases our love and does not drive us away.

Elder Jeffrey R. Holland said, "My desire today is for *all* of us, not just those who are 'poor in spirit,' but *all* of us—to have more straightforward personal experience with the Savior's example. Sometimes we seek heaven too obliquely, focusing on programs or history or the experience of others. Those are important but not as important as personal experience, true discipleship, and the strength that comes from experiencing firsthand the majesty of His touch."[24]

I once spoke with a young lady who was having a very difficult time forgiving herself and moving on. She had made some mistakes, and she said, "You don't understand, Sheldon. I knew what I did was wrong."

It is interesting that she said those specific words. Her statement is the very definition of sin—the fact that she knew that what she was doing was wrong, and she still did it. We know from the scriptures that all of us sin. All of us "come short of the glory of God" (Romans 3:23).

Her phrase makes me think of *Hymn* 194, "There Is a Green Hill Far Away." I love the line in that hymn that states, "He only could unlock the gate / Of heaven and let us in."

We need to try. We need to try as hard as we can, and even then it will not be enough without the Atonement of the Savior. He saves us, and He makes it, as Jacob says, so we do not have to become angels to a devil.

Elder Jeffrey R. Holland taught,

> To all of you who think you are lost or without hope, or who think you have done too much that was too wrong for too long, to every one of you who worry that you are stranded somewhere on the wintry plains of life and have wrecked your handcart in the process, this conference calls out Jehovah's unrelenting refrain, "[My] hand is stretched out still." "I shall lengthen out mine arm unto them," He said, "[and even if they] deny me; nevertheless, I will be merciful unto them, . . . if they will repent and come unto me; for mine arm is lengthened out all the day long, saith the Lord God of Hosts." His mercy endureth forever, and His hand is stretched out still. His is the pure love of Christ, the charity that never faileth, that compassion which endures even when all other strength disappears.[25]

Elder Bruce R. McConkie said, "Everyone in the Church who is on the straight and narrow path, who is striving and struggling and desiring to do what is right, *though [he] is far from perfect in this life*; if he passes out of this life while he's on the straight and narrow, *he's going to go on to eternal reward in his Father's kingdom.*"[26]

Doctrine and Covenants 45:3–5 states, "Listen to him who is the advocate with the Father, who is pleading your cause before him— Saying: Father, behold the sufferings and death of him who did no sin, in whom thou wast well pleased; behold the blood of thy Son which was shed, him whom thou gavest that thyself might be glorified. Wherefore, Father, spare these my brethren that believe on my name, that they may come unto me and have everlasting life."

ONE POSSIBLE CORRECT THOUGHT

I know I must expend my own best efforts, and my own best efforts will not be enough to save me, but if I rely on the Atonement of Jesus Christ, the Savior, He will save me.

When you start to feel inadequate and think, "I'm not good enough," "I can't do it," or "I'm doing my best, but I will still come up short," it is helpful to process this correct thought over and over. Even if we try our hardest, we are still not going to make it without the Savior. But when we do expend our own best efforts and we rely on the power of the Atonement, we can be saved in and through Him—only through Him.

Helpful Application Activity

The Lord is the perfect balance of justice and mercy. At times, this becomes difficult to apply in our own lives because we are not perfect at balancing justice and mercy. I have found that if individuals are overly anxious about their own salvation, they often only focus on the justice side of the Lord. Again, please remember this is not excusing or justifying sin, but we must understand that the Lord is full of truth and mercy, and it's easy to forget that. When you get caught in the trap of feeling unworthy no matter what, try to list the reasons the Lord, in His mercy, has accepted your offering; in other words, "tell the other side of the story."

For example, if someone has a difficult time forgiving him or herself, it might help to nurture thoughts such as, "I have spoken with the Lord's servant, and he worked me through a complete repentance process. I have felt the Spirit whisper to me multiple times that I was forgiven. I know through the Atonement that I can be saved."

This activity might help someone who has a hard time trusting the Lord better realize that we are "all hungry" and need to be "saved." When we learn to process the thoughts of a loving Savior, who has provided a way for us to return and become like Him and our Father, we are encouraged. Recognizing that we are fallen and "hungry" does not need to remain a frustration if we couple it with the majesty of the Atonement.

Principle 8 —
Learn to Be Content with What We Have Been Allotted

SITUATION

Mark's stake president knows Mark has served faithfully in his calling for nine years. Stake conference rolls around, and Mark is starting to wonder if he will receive a new calling. He pushes the thought aside, but by Sunday morning he feels sure a new calling will come. At conference, Mark sustains a new bishop, a new bishopric, a new stake president, a new stake presidency, and many new members of the high council. Mark is not called to any of these positions. He is interviewed later that day, and the bishop says, "I feel the Lord has asked you to serve as the Cub master." Mark thinks that maybe he did something wrong. He thinks maybe the Lord cannot trust him. He has a hard day.

Distorted Thought: The external validation I receive equals my actual worth.

External validation means that someone determines their worth because of callings, degrees, income, or athletic ability—things by which the world, and ofttimes we, perceive as our status.

I meet with a lot of individuals who feel they are important only if the world tells them they are important. They are important if they are rich, own a company, have a "prestigious" calling, are famous, are politically involved, and so on.

President Dieter F. Uchtdorf recently said,

> No calling is beneath us. Every calling provides an opportunity to serve and to grow. The Lord organized the Church in a way that offers each member an opportunity for service, which, in turn, leads to personal spiritual growth. Whatever your calling, I urge you to see it as

an opportunity not only to strengthen and bless others but also to become what Heavenly Father wants you to become. . . .

When we stand before the Lord to be judged, will He look upon the positions we have held in the world or even in the Church? Do you suppose that the titles we have had other than "husband," "father," or "priesthood holder" will mean much to Him? Do you think He will care how packed our schedule was or how many important meetings we attended? Do you suppose that our success in filling our days with appointments will serve as an excuse for failure to spend time with our wife and family?

The Lord judges so very differently from the way we do. He is pleased with the noble servant, not with the self-serving noble.[27]

President Uchtdorf acknowledges that the Lord and the world judge differently. The world will often look at career standing, wealth, prestige, beauty, and performing ability, and use these markers to determine someone's "worth." Throughout the history of time, however, the Lord has proven that none of that matters. He has done a marvelous work and wonder with a simple farm boy, Joseph Smith; has translated a city led by Enoch, who was "slow in speech"; and the examples go on.

At the conclusion of his talk, President Uchtdorf said,

There is a better way, taught to us by the Savior himself: "Whosoever will be chief among you let him be your servant."

When we seek to serve others, we are motivated not by selfishness but by charity. This is the way Jesus Christ lived his life and the way a holder of the priesthood must live his. The Savior did not care for the honors of men; Satan offered him all the kingdoms and glory of the world and Jesus rejected the offer immediately and completely. Throughout His life, the Savior must have often felt tired and pressed upon, with scarcely a moment to Himself; yet He always made time for the sick, the sorrowful, and the overlooked.[28]

President Uchtdorf makes a point here that I love. At the end of this life, the Lord is going to be less concerned with the external validation or things we have accomplished and is going to be more excited and pleased with us for the things we have done within our own families and within our hearts. He cares *how* we serve and not *where* we serve.

I remember I felt this principle even stronger one general conference when President Gordon B. Hinckley's son was sustained as a general authority and President Hinckley mentioned that his son's name was proposed through the proper channels like any other general authority. Elder Richard G. Hinckley, President Hinckley's son, mentioned at the next general conference that he might have been the only general authority to be sustained with a disclaimer.

In his "disclaimer," President Hinckley said,

> First I'd like to say just a word concerning those we have sustained this afternoon as members of the Quorum of the Seventy.
>
> I am convinced that there are *literally hundreds of brethren worthy and capable* to serve as general officers of the Church. We see them everywhere. Those sustained today have been chosen to fill particular responsibilities.[29]

I love that President Hinckley states that there are many people who can serve in these positions and that the Lord calls certain individuals for a particular reason. It does not mean that the other individuals who are not called are less able, worthy, qualified, or loved. In the grand plan of salvation, the Lord has many reasons for calling those He calls, when He calls them.

So if our external validation is not the real goal, then what is? Alma 29:1–3 gives great insight into what our true goal can and should be. Alma gives us a great example of how to measure our worth. He says, "O that I were an angel, and could have the wish of mine heart. . . . But behold, I am a man, and do sin in my wish."

It's important to point out that Alma recognizes his feelings are a sin. I have heard some people refer to this verse as Alma simply being humble, but I am going to believe Alma when he states that he feels he is sinning and should not want to be an angel because the Lord is not asking him to be an angel.

He goes on: "For I ought to be *content* with the things which the Lord hath *allotted* unto me" (Alma 29:3; emphasis added). So, if we are not supposed to aspire to things the Lord is not asking us to do, then what are we supposed to aspire to?

In Alma 29:9, Alma gives us the key. "Yea, and this is my glory, that perhaps I may be an *instrument* in the hands of God." Alma recognizes that we should all strive to be instruments in the hands of the Lord in whatever way He wants to use us.

We can see the importance of doctors using the right instruments. In surgery, a doctor needs to use a sharp, sterile scalpel, not a dull and dirty scalpel. Our job is to be the best instrument we can be so we are ready when the Lord needs us in whatever capacity that might be.

If we were a writing utensil, would we write what we want to write or refuse to write at all? Think about that. If we were the instrument, we would write exactly what the author wants us to write.

If we were a piano and the Lord the musician, we would not play the music we want to play; we would play the music He wants to play, and our job would be to reflect what He is playing. We are supposed to be *instruments* in the hands of God.

President Uchtdorf taught,

> I once owned a pen that I loved to use during my career as an airline captain. By simply turning the shaft, I could choose one of four colors. The pen did not complain when I wanted to use red ink instead of blue. It did not say to me, "I would rather not write after 10 p.m., in heavy fog, or at high altitudes." The pen did not say, "Use me only for important documents, not for the daily mundane tasks." With greatest reliability it performed every task I needed, no matter how important or insignificant. It was always ready to serve.
>
> In a similar way we are tools in the hands of God. When our heart is in the right place, we do not complain that our assigned task is unworthy of our abilities. We gladly serve wherever we are asked. When we do this, the Lord can use us in ways beyond our understanding to accomplish His work.[30]

One day many years ago, I prayed that I could be an instrument in the hands of the Lord. I was pondering this concept as I was leaving the gym, and as I drove home, I saw a man smoking a cigarette on the corner. I had an instant flashback and remembered I had gone with my bishop to visit this man years earlier. The visit had been brief and uneventful. On this particular day, I had an impression to stop and speak with him. I ignored the impression at first because I knew the man wouldn't remember me. I didn't want to come across as awkward or weird, so I continued to drive. The impression returned, so I made a U-turn and pulled up next to him.

I rolled down the window and said, "Hello, how are you?"

His response confirmed my anxieties. "Who are you?"

I told him I had visited him a few years ago with the bishop of our ward.

The man looked puzzled and said, "I remember the bishop."

I think what he really meant was that he remembered the bishop and had no clue who I was.

We spoke for a moment, and then I drove off. It did not seem earth-shattering, and I had my doubts about the visit, but as I drove away, this rebuke came to my heart and mind: "I thought you wanted to be an instrument." I learned in that moment, and try to continue to learn, that when I follow small and simple impressions from the Lord and know He is leading me, I should feel validated because I never know what His purposes may be.

There is possibly no better feeling than the assurance that the Lord has used you to further His work in some small way. It will be wonderful to one day see how the Lord used individuals in small ways to bring to pass a "marvelous work and wonder."

I love Paul's teaching regarding this subject. He states, "For as the body is one, and hath many members, and all the members of that one body, being many, are one body: so also is Christ. . . . And if the ear shall say, because I am not the eye, I am not of the body; is it therefore not of the body? If the whole body were an eye, where were the hearing? If the whole were hearing, where were the smelling?" (1 Cor. 12:12, 16–17).

Just as the body does not need every member to be an ear or a nose or the brain, the Lord does not need every member to be the bishop or to have a PhD or to be wealthy. We all have spiritual gifts. The Lord will use us all if we allow Him to do so. The feeling of knowing that we are on the Lord's errand is truly wonderful. And when we strive to be an instrument, to do whatever He wants us to do, we will have great joy and peace.

So what is our worth? A basic economic lesson may help us understand this concept. If I were to ask how much a regular baseball costs at a local sports store, what would you answer? Most people would guess two or three dollars.

What if I were to ask how much someone would pay for the Barry Bonds home-run ball that beat Hank Aaron's all-time home-run record? People are willing to pay hundreds of thousands, if not millions, of dollars for that ball. But it is still just a baseball. It always fascinates me that the ball was worth three dollars to begin with, and one swing of the bat made it worth millions. What is the difference? The way you define worth is what someone is willing to pay. Barry Bonds's home-run ball is worth a lot more because people are willing to pay more.

If we went to a sports store and they were selling baseballs for six hundred thousand dollars, no one would buy them. On the other hand, if they were going to sell Barry Bonds's home-run ball for three dollars, you would have a lot of bidders.

If you have ever tried to sell a house, you understand this principle well. An appraisal can say your house is worth two hundred and fifty thousand dollars, but unless someone is willing to pay that amount of money, it does not matter what the appraised value is.

So now we come to the question, what are we worth to the Savior? The follow-up question would be, "How much was He willing to pay?"

In Doctrine and Covenants 19, we get the only firsthand account of what happened in the Garden of Gethsemane. This section of scripture helps us begin to understand the price that was paid for you and for me. The Savior said, "For behold, I, God, have suffered these things for all, that they might not suffer if they would repent; Which suffering caused myself, even God, the greatest of all, to tremble because of pain, and to bleed at every pore, and to suffer both body and spirit—and would that I might not drink the bitter cup and shrink" (D&C 19:16, 18).

So how much did He pay? The answer is *everything*. He gave every part of His life and soul to save us. In fact, it is His work and His glory to bring to pass our immortality and our eternal life (see Moses 1:39).

If I were to buy Barry Bonds's baseball, I would not just throw it in the back of a closet. I would not lose it or throw it in the bucket of balls with the rest that I pitch to my sons while they hit. I would treat it differently because I paid so much and because it is worth so much.

Likewise, the Savior gave everything for every single one of us. Our worth to Him is great. The worth of souls is great in His sight because He paid so much. He is not going to throw us into the back of the closet. He paid way too much to do that.

I absolutely know that individuals who feel they are worth nothing will experience an increase of stress. I bear testimony that we can know we are important to Him, not by what our calling is or how many degrees we have or any other external marker but by how much He paid for us.

ONE POSSIBLE CORRECT THOUGHT

One day I will stand before the Lord and He will care more about how I have served than where I have served. I know I am worth everything to the Lord because of the price He paid for me. When I feel overwhelmed with external markers, I must refocus on being an instrument.

Whenever we seek validation from external sources, we are tempted to overcontrol the situation. When we seek validation from the Lord by being an instrument, we feel more encouraged.

HELPFUL APPLICATION ACTIVITY

Keep an instrument log. I know this may sound strange, but I have seen this simple process bless many people's lives. One of the major keys is that you keep this somewhat private. If you seek to be an instrument so you can tell everyone how great you are, this process stops being as effective. Obviously, when moved upon by the Spirit, you can share these types of experiences, but you should avoid going into this activity hoping to experience something so you can bring attention to yourself.

First, monitor how effective you are at remembering the principle of being an instrument. You may start by keeping track of how often you pray about this. It might help to hang a one-word sign on your mirror that says "Instrument." Or you can add this to your journal.

Once you are tracking, or remembering to be an instrument, begin noticing the small impressions the Lord sends. Maybe you feel impressed to call someone or stop by someone's house or send someone an e-mail. Maybe you feel prompted to look one more time for that address you could not find on the ward list.

As you take steps to be an instrument, start recording how the Lord is using you to further His work. This activity will help validate you, keep the experience between you and the Lord, and help you realize you don't need to hold a certain calling, status, or degree to begin immediately.

This process will help you remember your worth to the Lord because you will recognize He is working in your life.

Principle 9—

God Is Omniscient; Therefore, He Knows Everything

SITUATION

A mother says, "I'm not sure if buying this house is a good idea. The market is down, but you never know what's going to happen. I'm not sure if I should go back to school or not, because it might put us in a difficult position. It would be great to finish my degree, but I'm not sure I can do it. My husband was offered a job in a different state, but I worry if we move that the new location will not be the best place for my kids."

> *Distorted Thought: In order to feel secure, I need to know how everything is going to work out. The more aggressively I try to control the situation, and the more I plan every detail, the better my chances will be that things will work out that way.*

We do not know what is going to happen; we have no idea. In fact, it can cause a lot of stress when we try to control all of the factors to ensure that things will work out the way we want them to.

In this situation, the mother does not want to make any decisions because she doesn't know the outcome. I meet a lot of people who are paralyzed when faced with making decisions because they are afraid of the consequences. I am not referring to decisions about right and wrong; I am referring to the decisions that mortality forces on all of us—where to go to college, what to major in, whether to take a particular job, whether to invest in this option or that one.

These are hard decisions because we can't know how they'll turn out. That is part of why this life is so challenging and why we need to rely on our Heavenly Father, step out in faith, and do the best we can. No one knows the end from the beginning. Look at these scriptures. In 1 Nephi 11:17, notice what Nephi says: "Nevertheless, I *do not know the meaning* of all things" (emphasis added). Nephi didn't know the meaning of all things.

In Doctrine and Covenants 49:7, it says, "The day"—meaning the Second Coming—"*no man knoweth, neither the angels in heaven*" (emphasis added). It is saying that even angels do not know everything. So we are in good company in not knowing everything about the future.

Although we do not know everything, Heavenly Father, His Son, and the Holy Ghost do.

In 2 Nephi 9:20, it says, "There is not anything save he knows it." This verse is crucial to understand. If we have fear because we don't know the future, that fear can be replaced with the knowledge that the Lord does know everything. We don't have to know everything, because the Lord does. The Lord will often tell us the next step, and it is important to trust His instructions because we must always remember He also knows the last step. We do not need to know every single detail of our lives and how things are going to play out. All we need to do is rely on the Lord and seek His guidance for the next step.

In fact, Alma teaches clearly that "Faith is *not* to have a perfect knowledge of things" (Alma 32:21; emphasis added). It seems that an underlying principle of mortality is that we are *not* going to understand everything. Much like a young child learns to rely on his parents for information and comfort, we must rely on the Lord for guidance. The process of not knowing what comes next and learning to understand His will brings growth in our lives.

Joseph Smith said, "The great Jehovah contemplated the whole of the events connected with the earth, pertaining to the plan of salvation, before it rolled into existence. . . . He ordered all things according to the council of His own will. He knows the situation of both the living and the dead, and has made ample provision for their redemption, according to their several circumstances, and the laws of the kingdom of God, whether in this world, or in the world to come."[31]

Think about the importance of knowing that principle. Our Savior and Heavenly Father understand everything. All things are present before Them. They know the future and what is going to happen. Conversely, it can cause a lot of stress on our part when we don't know what is going to happen one, five, or twenty years down the road. So the way to lower our stress and anxiety about the future is to seek the guidance of our Savior and Heavenly Father.

One day I was sitting at the table with my son, trying to help him learn to read. He stumbled on some words, and I started worrying. I began to negatively predict the future and fill in the blanks for all of the challenges he was going to have if he couldn't read at grade level. I thought of every detail, all the way up to his career, if he couldn't read well enough.

Suddenly, I had a flashback. I was back in the second grade, and my teacher told me I was going to a different class. When I got there, I realized it was a class for kids who could not read at grade level. I was mortified. Even thinking about it now brings back those same feelings of shame and embarrassment. We started working on letters and sounds and reading skills, and it was terrible, and I was embarrassed. I felt bad as a little seven-year-old. I would go home to my mom and cry and cry. My mom pointed this out to my teacher and explained that I was having a hard time in the class, so my teacher decided to pull me out because of the negative feelings I was having. And here I am, years later, and guess what? I learned how to read, and I think I learned well enough. So there I was, sitting with my little son and beginning to fill in all the blanks on a life that had not happened yet, but remembering that time in my own childhood put things into perspective, and my stress level was lowered. I realized everything didn't hinge on this moment or this week or this year of my son's life. I was more patient, and I found out that if I was not as hard on my son, he made progress and read much better. This experience helped me better understand the perspective of Heavenly Father. He can offer peace because He knows how the end plays out.

On another day, I had a mother break down in my office. She had two daughters who were addicted to drugs, and the situation was consuming the emotional energy of the whole family. The mother had some legitimate concerns and doubts about the future. In that moment, I felt inspired to ask her, "Have you ever felt peace that things will work out?" She answered that she had felt moments of peace now and again. I felt impressed to ask another question. "If Heavenly Father knows everything—and He does—why would He send peace if there is no hope?"

In that moment, I also learned something. I do not know how everything will work out; however, I know we worship a God who knows everything. The more I turn to Him in my current stress, the more He can comfort me because He knows the end of the story. I am not suggesting that everything will work out the way we want it, but it will work out in ways that are best.

My wife, Nicole, has an ability to trust the Lord and believe that everything is going to work out. I am pretty high-strung at times, and I often start to fill in every unknown detail. In these moments, Nicole is able to calm me down and remind me to trust the Lord.

The Lord says in Doctrine and Covenants 6:36, "Look unto me in every thought; doubt not, fear not." I cannot say the same thing to my own son. He can't look to me with the same absolute faith and trust because there are many things I don't know. A lot of times all I can do is make my best guess with my limited knowledge. When we look to the Lord, however, we can have absolute confidence that He knows everything.

Some types of questions do not necessarily have a right and wrong answer. True, the Lord may send someone a personal impression to do something specific, but many questions do not have eternal principles that govern the answers.

It is important to remember that the concept of "choose the right" implies that there is an opposite "wrong choice." Sometimes the Lord allows us to use our agency and act. Obviously, if the Lord has specified a right choice through the scriptures and His prophets, we should follow. However, many decisions are within our power to make. If we treat every decision in life as a "right" or "wrong" question, we will become emotionally drained over time.

There have been many, many times in my life when I've felt that I've made a "wrong decision," but looking back years later, I've realized it was absolutely the perfect decision.

I remember going to Ricks College to play baseball my freshman year of college. I was certain I was going to be on the team. I had every indication from the coach and others that everything was going to work out.

One day, the coach pulled me into his office and said, "Hey, Sheldon, I think we're going to red-shirt you your freshman year so you can play for two years after your mission."

I was devastated, and I thought I had made the wrong decision to attend there. I wanted to play; I knew I could do it.

But I red-shirted that year and then left on my mission. I had been out about a year when I received the news that Ricks College was going to become BYU–Idaho. The switch entailed getting rid of their inner-collegiate athletic program. I still had an opportunity to return and play after my mission, but I prayed about that decision and felt I should apply to a different university.

To apply as a transfer student to the university I had chosen, I needed to have a certain number of credits, which I just barely had. And the reason

I had the right amount of credits was that I had red-shirted, which had allowed me to take two extra classes. At the time of red-shirting, I felt I had made the wrong choice, but when they announced the change, I was reassured I had made the choice the Lord wanted me to make. It is always important to remember the Lord knows more than we do.

When we feel anxious about a decision or an unknown outcome, remember that, one, we don't know everything; two, the Lord does; and three, we're probably making the best decision we can, and we can trust in the Lord. Doubt not and fear not.

If Heavenly Father knows everything, and we do not, then the need for revelation becomes paramount in our lives. President Boyd K. Packer said, "Every one of us can be guided by the spirit of revelation and the gift of the Holy Ghost."[32]

Elder Richard G. Scott has taught this principle clearly and often. He has said,

> Father in Heaven knew that you would face challenges and be required to make some decisions that would be beyond your own ability to decide correctly. In His plan of happiness, He included a provision for you to receive help with such challenges and decisions during your mortal life. That assistance will come to you through the Holy Ghost as spiritual guidance. It is a power, beyond your own capability, that a loving Heavenly Father wants you to use consistently for your peace and happiness. . . .
>
> What may appear initially to be a daunting task will be much easier to manage over time as you consistently strive to recognize and follow feelings prompted by the Spirit. Your confidence in the direction you receive from the Holy Ghost will also become stronger. I witness that as you gain experience and success in being guided by the Spirit, your confidence in the impressions you feel can become more certain than your dependence on what you see or hear.[33]

ONE POSSIBLE CORRECT THOUGHT

God knows everything, so I don't need to know how everything will work out. I will remember that He will help me through this. My part is to do my best to seek His will.

We do not need to know everything about the future to feel calm. We simply need to have confidence that the Lord does know everything and that as we seek His will we will be guided in the next step. One step is enough to move us forward.

Helpful Application Activity

Garth Brooks has a song titled "Unanswered Prayers." This song tells about how, at a certain point in life, he wanted something badly and prayed for it every night. Years later he realized those "unanswered prayers"—or more doctrinally accurate, "answered-differently-from-what-he-wanted prayers"—were a great blessing.

In therapy, I will sometimes use "coping" questions. These questions focus on past experiences when someone faced a similar challenge and worked through it successfully. Remembering these helps someone realize they can cope with a similar challenge they are currently facing.

Think of a time when you were uncertain about a decision, and at the time, it seemed as though things were not coming together.

Now replay in your mind the blessings that have come from that time and the events that followed. This process helps us remember that as we seek the Lord's guidance, He will lead us. The path may at times seem difficult, unknown, and scary, but if we remember that He helped us before, we will realize that He will help us again.

Principle 10 –

We Find What We Seek

In Doctrine and Covenants 88:63, it says, "Seek me diligently and ye shall find me."

SITUATION

I mention to a man named Jeff that our bishop is a good man. Jeff says, "Yes, but he could be a little more organized." I mention to Jeff that he looks nice in his new suit. Jeff says, "Yeah, but I'd look better if I lost thirty pounds." I mention to Jeff that his son gave a good talk in Primary. Jeff says, "I wish he'd clean up his room."

Distorted Thought: The negative events in my life equal all of the details of reality.

Let me give you an example, something I want you to imagine. I want you to imagine a big hourglass, and in the middle of that hourglass, a large filter. In a given day, all of the positives and negatives are piled into the top of this hourglass, and they start funneling down. This filter catches all of the positives, and releases the negatives. If you focus only on the negative things in life because they are all piled together at the bottom of the hourglass, you are naturally going to feel a little more anxious. This is distorted, though, because there are positives and negatives in virtually every given situation. You can't just stop on the bad when there is most likely just as much good at the same time.

We depend on perspective. If I were to take you to a football field and say, "Look!" your next question would probably be, "For what?" When we look, we look *for* something. In French, there are separate verbs for "to look" and "to look for," but in English, we use those verb equivalents interchangeably and understand the difference through context. If I had lost my wallet on the football field, you would look at the field differently than if we were bird watching.

Here's the principle: You find what you're looking for.

If I lost my keys in my house and I turned my kids loose to find them, instead of looking for keys, they would probably look for LEGOs. And they would probably find LEGOs because they would be looking for them. We find what we are looking for.

Nephi may be one of the most gifted individuals in finding the positive in each situation. 1 Nephi 17:2 says, "And so great were the blessings of the Lord upon us, that while we did live upon raw meat in the wilderness, our women did give plenty of suck for their children, and were strong, yea, even like unto the men; and they began to bear their journeyings without murmurings."

These statements are absolutely remarkable. Nephi and his family have to eat raw meat, and he perceives it as a blessing. That perspective is a true gift.

My wife, Nicole, and I tried to set a world record one month for how many appliances and vehicles we could break, and I think we came pretty close to a new record.

First, our water heater broke . . . Well, I should qualify that; I broke the water heater, and I learned something from that experience. My neighbor said, and I quote, "You cannot mess *this* up." I have now taken that to mean, "Call a professional," because that's what I should have done, even though I was just trying to clean it.

Around that same time, our washer broke, our van died on a trip in California, then our second car also broke down, and the ice maker in the fridge stopped working. I know the pioneers could hardly look at a broken ice maker as a trial, but all of this was frustrating to us. If we would have focused on everything that was breaking, I bet you could guess how we would have felt. However, after a few weeks we started to notice that with every bad situation came a good outcome. Our water heater broke, but we had a neighbor who was a plumber, and he came over and helped me; well, he actually just fixed it himself. My role was to watch. And he wouldn't let us pay him.

A few weeks after returning from California, we were able to find a new van within our price range, and the dealer was able to use our broken-down van in California as a trade-in. Another neighbor helped with the second broken-down car, and we started to realize the water heater, the washer, and the cars were our "raw meat" experiences. We didn't like what had happened, but we started to notice the blessings that came from each one because of good neighbors and friends.

I think just about anyone could easily list the negatives about life. For most, it's hard to find positives. For some, it can be hard because they go through really challenging experiences. But every situation has both positive and negative, and when you try to focus on the good, it doesn't mean you ignore the negatives or pretend they don't exist; it simply means you start to process the Lord's tender mercies in your life, and often, you feel better.

We must learn to search for and find the positive. If we do not search for the positive, then the negative feelings may lead to anger or frustration. But there are other options besides anger and frustration when you're dealing with a stressful situation. Laughter may be one of the best antidotes. Elder Joseph B. Wirthlin told how he and his family chose to laugh when faced with being lost on a road trip as well as with many other trying times in their lives. He said,

> There is an antidote for times such as these: learn to laugh.
>
> Instead of getting angry, we laughed . . . Every time we made a wrong turn, we laughed harder.
>
> Getting lost was not an unusual occurrence for us. Once while heading south to Cedar City, Utah, we took a wrong turn and didn't realize it until two hours later when we saw the "Welcome to Nevada" signs. *We didn't get angry. We laughed*, and as a result, anger and resentment rarely resulted. Our laughter created cherished memories for us.[34]

Elder Wirthlin tells of another example:

> I remember when one of our daughters went on a blind date. She was all dressed up and waiting for her date to arrive when the doorbell rang. In walked a man who seemed a little old, but she tried to be polite. She introduced him to me and my wife and the other children; then she put on her coat and went out the door. We watched as she got into the car, but the car didn't move. Eventually our daughter got out of the car and, red faced, ran back into the house. The man that she thought was her blind date had actually come to pick up another of our daughters who had agreed to be a babysitter for him and his wife.

We all had a good laugh over that. In fact, we couldn't stop laughing. Later, when our daughter's real blind date showed up, I couldn't come out to meet him because I was still in the kitchen laughing. Now, I realize that our daughter could have felt humiliated and embarrassed. But *she laughed* with us, and as a result, *we still laugh* about it today.

The next time you're tempted to groan, you might try to laugh instead. It will extend your life and make the lives of all those around you more enjoyable.[35]

President Thomas S. Monson is a great example of learning not to take yourself too seriously. He said,

> If I might add a personal touch, I share with you an experience that embarrassed, a game that was lost, and a *lesson in not taking ourselves too seriously.*
>
> First, in a basketball game when the outcome was in doubt, the coach sent me onto the playing floor right after the second half began. I took an in-bounds pass, dribbled the ball toward the key, and let the shot fly. Just as the ball left my fingertips, I realized why the opposing guards did not attempt to stop my drive: I was shooting for the wrong basket! I offered a silent prayer: "Please, Father, don't let that ball go in." The ball rimmed the hoop and fell out.
>
> From the bleachers came the call: "We want Monson, we want Monson, we want Monson—*out!*" The coach obliged.
>
> I never was a basketball star.[36]

When we look closer at this story, we can see how President Monson could have chosen to be embarrassed or angry at this mistake. But he was not. He decided not to take himself too seriously.

I know what you might be thinking: "We're just supposed to laugh when life gets hard?"

Well, yes. You are.

I will often draw a forked road on the whiteboard in my office when meeting with clients. At the fork, I will write the situations that are causing stress. I will point out to my clients that the situation happened—it's done.

That part cannot be changed. And then I invite them to, instead, focus on the direction they are going.

If Nicole and I could have laughed earlier about our situation with the broken appliances or if we could have seen the blessings earlier, I think we would have felt better sooner. We would have opened ourselves up to seeing the tender mercies of the Lord instead of being blinded by self-pity and frustration.

Is laughter the only answer? No. But it is a reality that we can choose how we are going to view stressful situations and how we are going to deal with them. I wish I could be more like Elder Wirthlin and laugh when I get lost. I often do not. I get frustrated, and I start to feel that "as the dad," I should know the way. My thoughts make me frustrated, and I often end up angry.

Wouldn't I be better off to see the "Nevada sign" in my life and laugh? If I look for the negative, I know I can find it, and if I continue to focus on it, I know I will feel worse.

One year I tried to learn to snowboard with the priests in our ward. Having grown up in California, this was a skill I had not acquired. After a few times, I was able to get up and go down the hill slowly. I had a hard time staying on the slope. I wouldn't fall, but I couldn't go where I wanted to go.

A friend of mine gave me some priceless advice: "Quit looking at where you do not want to go, and focus on where you want to go. Your body will follow." This advice can be applied in life's arena as well as the slope.

If you focus your energy on the negative aspects about life, you will end up with a negative experience. If you focus on the positives and the blessings, you will end up with a positive experience. Make the choice to focus on where you really want to go and laugh at stressful situations.

ONE POSSIBLE CORRECT THOUGHT

There are positives and negatives about every situation. When I search for and find the positives, I will feel better.

Remember that you will find what you are looking for. As you look for the blessing and the hand of the Lord, you will find it.

HELPFUL APPLICATION ACTIVITY

Look at the following picture and decide which line is longer:

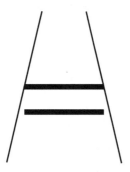

Look at this picture and decide which line is longer:

In the first picture, the lines are identical. In the second, the lines are also identical. The only reason one looks bigger than the other in the second picture is that our perspective has changed. It is interesting how we have an ability to look at life from a different perspective. Choose to look at a situation with hope, love, and optimism. Choose to laugh and not take yourself too seriously.

As a helpful reminder, if one of my clients is struggling with this principle, I have them put two lines on their mirror as a reminder of perspective. You might want to do the same if you have a hard time with this principle.

Principle 11 –
Learn to Remove Comparisons

SITUATION

Billy is feeling anxious and can't figure out why. After a few hours, he realizes why he might be feeling down. Billy went to dinner with some old friends from college the night before. His old college roommate is a bishop, makes great money, and is in great shape. Billy realizes that his friend never said anything to compare their different situations, but he's felt anxious since that dinner.

Distorted thought: If that person succeeds, then I've failed.

President Ezra Taft Benson taught clearly that the concept of "if you succeed, I am a failure" is a prideful thought.[37] How should we feel when someone else succeeds? The Lord wants everyone to succeed and do well.

In Romans 8:17, we learn about the Lord's personality. This verse states, "And if children, then heirs; heirs of God, and joint-heirs with Christ; if so be that we suffer with him, that we may be also glorified together."

Joint-heirs with Christ? What in the world could you or I ever do to merit the same reward as our Lord and Master?

Do you see His personality there? If there was ever a person who could feel cheated if someone else received the same reward as Him, it would be the Savior. The Savior's Atonement is the greatest event in the history of this universe. To suggest that you or I could do anything to receive a reward similar to His seems almost blasphemous.

We learn, however, that the Savior wants to raise everyone to His level and does not view this as a competition. He doesn't want us to just "make it"; He wants us to have everything He has, even though He did more than we did. He did it perfectly, but He still wants us to get the same reward. He absolutely and wholeheartedly wants others to succeed.

President Dieter F. Uchtdorf said, "My beloved fellow disciples of the gentle Christ, should we not hold ourselves to a higher standard? As priesthood bearers, we must realize that all of God's children wear the same jersey. Our team is the brotherhood of man. This mortal life is our playing field. Our goal is to learn to love God and to extend that same love toward our fellowman. We are here to live according to his law and establish the kingdom of God. We are here to build, uplift, treat fairly, and encourage all of Heavenly Father's children."[38]

I love competitive sports, but we need to understand that life is not a competition. In Father's plan, all can win. He will allow as many to win as want to play by the rules. There does not have to be a loser just because there is a winner. He wants everyone to succeed, and we should seek to bring others up with us.

I have met individuals who see others' successes as their failure. I knew a woman who got caught up in what I call the "Christmas Card Effect." In a Christmas card, families will always put their best foot forward. There is nothing wrong with this, but some people see others' successes as evidence that they themselves are accomplishing nothing.

This sweet sister spent much of her day reading the Facebook posts of her friends. I am sure you have seen some of these "Christmas Card" posts, things such as, "I just love spending time with my beautiful children," "My friends love me so much. They are the best," and "My husband loves me so much. He bought me a new purse." Now, there is nothing wrong with posting these types of things, but someone who has a "you succeed, I fail" attitude will see them and think, *I get frustrated with my kids, my friends don't call me*, and *my husband and I don't get each other anything*.

Isn't it amazing that someone else sharing a success in their life can make us feel anxious? I have met parents who have encouraged certain children to not share a success in life for fear of hurting the other siblings' feelings. We must learn and remember that we are on the same team. If a sibling gets a raise, degree, new home, or new furniture, it is not an attack on you.

I knew a man who had a difficult time handling a new boss who was younger than he was. This younger boss was this man's friend but had been promoted above him. The boss was talented, worked hard, had a personality for leadership, and was diligent. The older employee began to believe that he had somehow failed.

This employee was talented in his field. He was one of the top employees in the company. He was a team player, worked hard, was diligent and organized, and really loved his job. On this occasion, however, he felt he had completely failed because his friend was made the new boss. Think of the emotional weight that could have been lifted had this man been genuinely happy that his friend received the position. Think of what type of employee and help he could have been to the new boss.

I am absolutely certain that each of you has witnessed a situation where you've understood why one person was chosen over another—and the reason was not ability. I am sure you have seen this at work, in the Church, and in the family when someone has been given an opportunity because of the situation and not because of the stature.

I have many heroes in the gospel, but some of my favorite characters in Church history and the scriptures are the background individuals who never viewed life as a competition—the Hyrum Smiths, Sams, and Oliver Grangers of the world.

My favorite scriptural story of background characters is the story of the two thousand sixty stripling warriors. One of the reasons I love this story is that we never know their names. I am sure these young men had different personalities, abilities, and strengths, but we identify them only as a group.

I am guessing that in the heat of battle, some of the warriors did heroic things to save one another's lives, but all we know is that all of them fought and none died. Wouldn't this be a great motto for wards, stakes, missions, and for the Church? Wouldn't it be wonderful to say that the Church in the twenty-first century fought as one and came off conqueror?

We are all given different opportunities for different reasons. This life is not a competition among God's children; in fact, the only struggle we face is a battle over which team we are on. And it's not even about which team will win. That has already been determined. We just need to pick our side. In the Bible Dictionary under "Revelation of John," there is a wonderful sentence: "The message of Revelation is the same as that of all scripture: there will be an eventual triumph on this earth of God over the devil."[39]

The kingdom of God will prevail. The most important thing is not how good we are compared to those around us but whether we are fighting on God's team alongside those around us. We must choose the Lord, work to build His kingdom, and raise everyone up to be with us.

ONE POSSIBLE CORRECT THOUGHT

Like the Savior, I should be happy when others succeed and remember the battle is between good and evil—not between me and someone else. We're all on the same team. When someone else has success in their life, we should congratulate them. It doesn't mean we have failed or somehow come up short; it just means they've had a good turn and we will have one too when it's our time.

Helpful Application Activity

This activity is called "game tape." You are probably familiar with sports teams that replay the game tape to see the good and bad about a previous game. Teams also do this to watch and study their upcoming opponents.

In these moments, teams will often slow down the tape and point out remarkable plays that would otherwise go unnoticed in full speed. Often, a lineman blocks on a big yardage gain, or a basketball player switches and covers the pick-and-roll extremely well. These types of plays are often unnoticed by the average fan, but they are as crucial as any other play that happens.

You can use this analogy to help you notice things that may otherwise go unnoticed. You don't even have to tell the person. If we have in our mind that the Lord is building His kingdom and that miracles happen every day to further His work, then we have a lot to look for.

Look for how the Lord uses others as His instruments. It is even fun to document these events. For example, if your bishop gives a talk that seems like it was written for you, thank Heavenly Father for using the bishop to further the kingdom. If you notice someone has an attribute that will be extremely helpful to them in a new calling, thank Heavenly Father for this great opportunity for them. Over time you will begin to see these small things as witnesses and miracles that the Lord is using all of us to further His kingdom. You will also see that He uses people for different reasons and at different times.

The Lord will use all of the abilities He has given us to further His work. If we look around, we start to realize that there are no coincidences in the kingdom of God. He leads the work—and if we are making ourselves available, we will begin to see His tender mercies in our lives as well.

Principle 12 –
Avoid Mind Reading

SITUATION

Sister Johnson calls Sister Smith on the phone to discuss some Relief Society business. Sister Johnson can tell that Sister Smith is upset—probably at her. Sister Johnson does not know why Sister Smith is angry. She has been upset lately. She's probably angry because Sister Johnson didn't do her visiting teaching. But if Sister Smith only knew what kind of month Sister Johnson had had, she would get off her back.

> *Distorted Thought: Without anyone saying it, you know what others are thinking and feeling about you—you're absolutely convinced that you know. You're able to pick up on what they're communicating.*

Why is that distorted? We communicate in so many different ways, and because of that, it is difficult to know what others are thinking or feeling about us.

In Doctrine and Covenants 78:17, the Lord reminds us, "Verily, verily, I say unto you, ye are little children, and ye have not as yet understood."

We do not know every situation. There is danger in reacting negatively to partial information because although we are *certain* we understand, we are often wrong.

Have you ever seen a situation where someone did not know all of the facts, so they filled in the blanks and started a rumor mill?

A man recently came back to activity in the Church. The bishop and others rallied around this man to help him feel welcome in the ward. Not long after the man started attending church again, there was a baby blessing, and the father of the baby had previously invited this man to stand in the circle. The man, however, happened to be wearing a blue shirt. He walked up to the circle, and the bishop leaned over and whispered in his ear, after which the man returned to his seat.

Individuals who witnessed this began to fill in the blanks. "The bishop has no right to tell someone they can't bless a baby because they're wearing a blue shirt." "This man recently returned to activity, and even if that were the policy, the bishop should remember the spirit of the law." The rumors grew in intensity and frequency. Some ward members even started a campaign about why this bishop was wrong.

Here's what really happened. The bishop knew the situation of this man, and when the man got up to participate in the blessing, the bishop whispered to him, "You need the Melchizedek priesthood to bless a baby." The man apologized. "Oh, I'm sorry, Bishop." The bishop responded, "It's okay, don't worry about it." And the man went back to his seat.

See what really happened? Nothing! Nothing happened. We are really bad at mind reading. Individuals who start to mind read often come in for therapy feeling very anxious. The story often sounds like the following: "I just know my boss hates me." "I just know my wife is mad at me." "My mother-in-law doesn't like me because I'm not good enough for her."

Individuals become convinced that members of their ward, neighborhood, or family are thinking and feeling something about them, when, in reality, the perceived offender has no ill feelings.

I know a man who taught institute at prison for years. Interestingly enough, he began every class by saying, "Do not tell me what you did to get here." He explained that if he wanted to teach a lesson on honesty and they were in prison for being dishonest, he did not want them to think he was trying to speak directly to them because he knew what they did.

This tells us a lot about human nature. My friend wanted to teach the gospel without anyone thinking he had an agenda. I believe he did it this way because too often we fill in the blanks with our perceptions, not the facts.

He said he knew some of the people were in prison for drugs, but he didn't want to know which ones because if he was going to teach the Word of Wisdom, he was going to teach it the way the Lord wanted without worrying about whether some felt he was attacking them.

Perception is a fascinating subject. Two people can observe the exact same situation and see it differently. And to all of us, our perception is our reality. We must learn to bridle our perceptions and remember that we do not have all of the information.

If you drive down the road and wave at your bishop and he doesn't wave back, it doesn't mean he is shunning you because you missed your visiting teaching this month. He might not have seen you, he might have had something in his hand, he might have been thinking about the suicidal teen in the ward, or he might have been thinking about making it to his son's basketball game on time. He might have been running late to a meeting, or maybe his right arm was temporarily paralyzed because of a virus. The odds of his intentionally trying to shun you are low, so slow down and think about other possibilities.

How should we react if someone perceives that we are angry with them? We have a wonderful example in the Book of Mormon. Captain Moroni writes a very pointed and accusatory letter to Pahoran. In it, he states, "Yea, great has been your neglect towards us. And now behold, we desire to know the cause of this exceedingly great neglect; yea, we desire to know the cause of your thoughtless state. Can you think to sit upon your thrones in a state of thoughtless stupor, while your enemies are spreading the work of death around you?" (Alma 60:5–7).

In the next chapter of the Book of Mormon, Pahoran responds to Moroni's letter. He writes, "And now, in your epistle you have censured me, but it mattereth not; I am not angry, but do rejoice in the greatness of your heart" (Alma 61:9).

Moroni does not completely understand Pahoran's situation. Pahoran realizes this and does not become angry. He responds by helping Moroni understand his situation and receives in return an appreciative response from Moroni. Later, as we learn in Alma 62, Moroni marches to Pahoran's aid.

This story is helpful for many reasons. It is important to remember that we often do not understand everything about a situation and that our perception is not always reality. Secondly, when others' perceptions are wrong, we can choose to not get angry with them. We can rejoice in their "greatness of heart."

I have met with too many individuals who "know" something they really do not know. When they begin to fill in the blanks, and they have an anxious personality, it gives them a very negative view of the world.

If someone does something you interpret as them being upset with you, here are a few things to remember: One, you can't control what other people do, and two, you're probably not even correct in your interpretation. They might be saying or doing something that has nothing to do with your perception. You may interpret their action as meaning something they absolutely did not intend.

One Possible Correct Thought

We communicate in a variety of ways. People act a certain way for a variety of reasons, and I am only able to gather a small fraction of information.

Although we may think we know why people do and say certain things, we often do not. There are so many reasons surrounding others' actions and words that we need to remember we have a fraction of the information we need to make accurate judgments. Hopefully, we can learn that we do not understand completely why some individuals do and say certain things, because if we start to fill in the blanks about someone else's motives, we will feel an increase of worry.

Helpful Application Activity

If you find yourself filling in the blanks too often, slow down and replay the story. There are many possible options to every situation. It is helpful to replay these situations and remember the alternatives.

For example, if you think your bishop intentionally ignored you, take a moment to replay the scenario and think of other possibilities. Maybe he had just had a serious conversation and his mind was elsewhere. Maybe he was distracted by something else going on. Maybe he saw the youth in the hall and was wondering why they were not in Sunday School. Maybe he didn't hear you. This process can go on for a while. But remember that it is important to slow down and realize that our one perception is a possible reason but maybe not *the* reason.

Conclusion

BE STILL MY SOUL

I love the words of the hymn, "Be Still My Soul." As you read the words, think back to the many principles we have covered. This hymn begins to take on more meaning for me when I realize that we are singing about *how* to "be still."

> *Be still, my soul; The Lord is on thy side;*
> *With patience bear thy cross of grief or pain.*
> *Leave to thy God to order and provide;*
> *In ev'ry change he faithful will remain.*
> *Be still, my soul: Thy best, thy heav'nly Friend*
> *Thru thorny ways leads to a joyful end.*
>
> *Be still, my soul: Thy God doth undertake*
> *To guide the future as he has the past.*
> *Thy hope, thy confidence let nothing shake;*
> *All now mysterious shall be bright at last.*
> *Be still, my soul: The waves and winds still know*
> *His voice who ruled them while he dwelt below.*
>
> *Be still, my soul: The hour is hast'ning on*
> *When we shall be forever with the Lord,*
> *When disappointment, grief, and fear are gone,*
> *Sorrow forgot, love's purest joys restored.*
> *Be still, my soul: When change and tears are past,*
> *All safe and blessed we shall meet at last.*[40]

That hymn takes on more meaning when I realize how constant Christ truly is.

Personal Ministry

I would like to share a personal note about this book. Elder Neal A. Maxwell had a private ministry he felt he needed to engage in to help those struggling through leukemia.

His biography says something about him that has often inspired me: "Now that circle kept growing as Neal began to drop other after hours activities in favor of staying close to more people whose sorrows he now understood better than he ever could before."

In talking about those he would visit in the hospital, it says, "Neither Neal nor his Brethren, each of whom has his *own private ministry of some kind*, can do all that they wish were possible, but Latter-day Saints generally understand that the gifts of healing and blessing are not confined to Church leaders; they are gifts and priesthood privileges spread among all true disciples."[41]

I am in no way comparing myself to Elder Maxwell, but I have felt very much *a private ministry* in my life for those who have anxious souls.

I would like to share a personal experience with you to express my feelings about dealing with anxiety.

I served my mission in Paris, France, and loved every single minute of it. I didn't know what to call it then, but looking back, I think there was a part of my mission when I had excessive anxiety, even though naming it is probably not as important as understanding what I was feeling.

About a year into my mission, I started to feel overwhelmed, and I started to feel all of my weaknesses pressing on me every single day. I replayed every negative thing about myself over and over again. I became less patient with myself, and I started to get down on myself for every little mistake. I felt down and depressed, and I don't think anyone else in my mission knew.

I talked to my mission president about it, and he encouraged me. Much of what was going on was that I had started to realize how amazing the Lord and His kingdom were and how insignificant I was. The gap between the two became crushing at times. I taught people about the Atonement, but I had not learned how to apply it personally.

About two weeks before I came home, I hit one of the lowest moments I'd ever had. We had a mission rule that we were supposed to contact or bring up the gospel with someone every time we got on a bus, metro, or train. At this particular time, I didn't feel like contacting anyone but found the strength through obedience to contact the woman sitting next to me.

I would love to tell you that she was a "golden" contact. I would love to tell you that she joined the Church. That would make a wonderful *Ensign* article, wouldn't it?

But that's not what happened. She was possibly the rudest individual who had ever spoken to me in the entire two years of my mission. She insulted me, she insulted my religion, and she insulted my country—she insulted everything about me.

The woman spoke loudly enough that most of the train could hear her, and she even laughed at me before she got up and walked off the train.

Well, that experience didn't help much. We got to our stop, I looked down at my watch, and I realized we were going to be late. It was 9:23, and it was about a ten-minute walk to our apartment. It was a mission rule that we needed to be home by 9:30, and we weren't going to make it.

For the first time in my mission, I had the thought, *I don't care. I don't care tonight that I'm going to be late.*

I started to walk home, feeling very discouraged. I remember thinking, *I shouldn't feel like this. I have been serving a mission; I think I should feel differently.*

Walking back through the streets of Paris, feeling very low, something happened.

I can't explain exactly what happened, but this feeling started to grow in my heart. I started to run. I don't know if there were angels speaking by the power of the Holy Ghost or if it was the Holy Ghost Himself, but I had this feeling start to grow in my heart until a thought came as a clear voice to my heart and mind that said, "Keep running, my son, keep running. Don't you dare give up."

I felt more than the need to run home to our apartment. To me, those words meant, "Keep pushing through life, keep going because there are so many great days ahead." I felt that the Lord was speaking to me.

I ran and I ran, and when we arrived home, it was 9:29. We'd made it. My companion went to make a snack, and I went in the other room. I knelt down and had one of the neatest experiences I've ever had with the Lord. I felt a cleansing and a remission of my sins.

I learned a great lesson that night: that Jesus Christ is the Prince of Peace, the King of Kings, and that we must return to thoughts of Him and His Atonement often because anxious feelings will return, but we can overcome them through Christ's intervention in our lives.

I know that thoughts lead to feelings. Distorted thoughts lead to anxiety. Thoughts of the Atonement and Christ's gospel lead to peace.

I know He can heal every sickness. I know His Atonement can heal effectively and repeatedly throughout our entire lives and not just in a one-time event.

Clients often ask me why the Lord would allow them to feel so many anxious thoughts. I often think of John 9:2, where Christ's disciples ask, "Master, who did sin, this man, or his parents, that he was born blind?"

We think of that now and probably see it as ridiculous to draw the connection that someone could be born blind because of a former sin, and yet, with mental health challenges today, we often ask a similar question: if someone is anxious or depressed, who is to blame, the parents for raising them a certain way or the person because their feelings are connected to some type of wrong behavior?

Notice what the Savior says in John 9:3: "Jesus answered, Neither hath this man sinned, nor his parents: but that the works of God should be made manifest in him."

I know that sometimes we have a tendency, if we're having a bad day—which we're going to have—and if we're going through difficult things, to say, "Well, who sinned? Who messed up?" "Why are you worrying about life?" "Was it you, was it your parents, was it your family?" "What happened?"

I bear testimony that we have weaknesses so that the works of God can be made manifest in the Savior. Through these weaknesses, we are drawn to Him. I thank the Lord for a heart that can sometimes turn to anxiety, because through sacred and personal experiences, I have found His healing power in ways I never would have otherwise. I know as we turn to Him, we can find peace.

I know that when we take the sacrament and when we learn that we cannot change the past, we can remember that direction is important. We need to go forward.

I know that we will find peace when we learn not to look beyond the mark but to focus on the Savior. He *is* the mark; He is what we need to be shooting for.

I testify that anxiety will be reduced when we learn to find joy in the journey and remember that in every stage of life there are difficult experiences, but there is joy in every single day, and we will find it if we look for it.

I know that as we become more righteous, it does not guarantee that others are going to like us.

We can find peace as we learn not to negatively predict future events.

Our hearts will be comforted as we learn that it is by grace that we are saved and only through the atoning blood of Jesus Christ.

Anxiety will decrease when we learn to be content with the things the Lord has asked us to do and with the things He has allotted unto us.

Our peace will increase when we understand that He knows everything and that we don't need to know it all if we trust Him.

I know we will find what we seek, so we must seek Him, and we will find Him.

As we remove comparison in our lives and realize it is not a competition between us and others, we'll feel more at peace.

If we can avoid mind reading and stop feeling we know why others do and say the things they do and say, we will feel less anxiety.

I know that as we remember these principles and learn to process them over and over again, we can and will find peace in life.

I want to add my testimony to those that have been born before. I know with all of my heart that the Lord Jesus Christ lives and loves us. He wants to bless us and help us. I know when we process correct gospel principles, our feelings can move from fear to faith, from petrified to peaceful, and from anxiety to adoration. "He lives! He lives who once was dead."[42] Thoughts of Him will always lead to a more peaceful heart.

Appendix

THE BIG THREE—SLEEP, EXERCISE, AND DIET

Reframing cognitive distortions is a major factor in learning to manage excessive worry and anxiety. Along with repeated practice in readjusting these thoughts, we must also approach these challenges from a physical standpoint. I would like to discuss the big three things you can do to help with managing anxiety—sleep, diet, and exercise.

SLEEP

In Doctrine and Covenants 88:124, the Lord says, "Retire to thy bed early, that ye may not be weary; arise early, that your bodies and your minds may be invigorated."

Almost without fail, when someone comes in feeling anxious, I ask, "How are you sleeping?" and their answer is, "Not well."

When the mind is racing, it is difficult to sleep, but some people don't do themselves any favors when it comes to sleep.

I don't claim to be a sleep expert in any way, but I have observed hundreds of clients with sleep problems. It is important to remember that the body has natural cycles. It naturally starts to shut down and naturally starts to wake up. If you try to go to sleep when your body starts to shut down, you have higher odds of completing a healthy sleep cycle and feeling better.

The body and its mental state are closely related because if the brain is not given adequate time to rest, your level of resistance is lowered when dealing with stressful situations, and it's easier to feel anxious.

EXERCISE

The Lord tells us to cease to be idle. The natural chemicals your body releases when exercising help calm your nerves and help you deal with anxiety. Exercise is a great way to release endorphins to help fight against some of the difficult feelings and thoughts you have. I suggest to all of my clients, whatever their challenges, that they develop some type of exercise program. Does that mean bodybuilders and runners are not stressed? No. It simply means this is an important cog in the wheel.

Diet

Proper diet is an effective tool when dealing with anxiety. Doctrine and Covenants 89:11 says to eat "every herb in the season thereof, and every fruit in the season thereof." Notice that the Lord instructs us to eat foods in their season. In our day, we can eat fruits and vegetables virtually year-round.

However, I think there can be an underlying principle in this commandment. Fruits and vegetables *have* a season. We have a lot of food at our disposal today that does not have a season. Some processed foods can sit on the shelf for years and still be edible.

If food doesn't break down easily outside the body, it will be harder for the body to break it down inside. When food breaks down properly, our body is in better rhythm. Healthy eating helps the body deal with excessive anxiety in a healthy way.

A Word about Medication

I see too many people who refuse to speak with a medical professional about anxiety medication because they want to do it on their own. Some people need the assistance of anxiety medication, and some work through it without medication, but to suggest that somehow taking medication makes you less of a person, disciple, or member of the Church is inaccurate.

Can you imagine telling someone who wears glasses to have more faith and to pray more, and they will not need glasses? Can you imagine telling someone who had diabetes to stop taking medication because all they need is faith? We need to understand that medical advances exist in the mental health world, and they are there for our good when used properly. However, prescription medication abuse is on the rise, so please work closely with a trained medical professional.

I encourage any of you who wonder about the benefits of medication to meet with a qualified medical professional and ask questions. Ask your doctor all of the questions that concern you. If your doctor feels like medication would be beneficial, please consider that professional advice. Be open with your doctor. People respond differently to different medications. Share your concerns, worries, or side effects, and work with your doctor to achieve the best solution.

Please do not think that individuals who take anxiety or antidepressant medication are subpar. It is not true; such a thought is inappropriate.

SPIRITUAL HELPS

Here are some spiritual tips. The Lord asks us to serve Him with all of our "minds." I think that does apply to memorizing scriptures, getting an education, and studying. But I also think it means focusing your mind and not allowing it to go idle or to constantly process distorted thoughts. Push yourself to be aware of the things you are thinking. We must learn to act and not be acted upon. Thoughts lead to feelings, and anxious, distorted thoughts lead to anxious feelings.

All of the correct thoughts we have discussed are important to process. The Lord tells us, "Be still and know that I am God" (D&C 101:16). We live in a world that makes it difficult to be still, with opportunities to text, watch TV, surf the Internet, or spend time on Facebook; we have a lot of "screen time." That's not necessarily a bad thing; it's just part of the world that we live in, and some of those things are fine in moderation. But it is important that we take time to learn to be still. We can be still in the temple, while studying our scriptures, during sacrament meeting, and so on.

I am amazed at how many individuals who are feeling a little stressed or worried never take time to pray, let alone to just sit and be still for ten minutes in a day. They never think to unwind a bit. Often, their routine is something like this: alarm goes off, get up, take a shower; go to work, sit at the computer all day, drive home through traffic with the radio going; get home to watch TV, respond to e-mails, then hit the sack. There is never a time where we just sit. We must set aside time in the day to be still.

As you finish this book, you will set it down and all of the triggers for anxiety and negative thinking that have plagued you before will come back again. May I make a few closing suggestions.

First, learn to control your thoughts. What you think will lead to how you feel. If you hope to lessen worry without addressing your thoughts, you will face an uphill battle.

Second, some of the principles in this book probably hit home more closely than others. Start with those things that are most pressing. When you feel you are improving, you can then tackle another distorted thought. But remember to be patient with yourself.

Third, reread this book. Our lives change, and it is important to review principles often to continue to improve.

Fourth, and most important, resolve in your mind that the Savior and His gospel are the answer. He is the answer. Drawing closer to the Lord is the most peaceful pursuit we can undertake. He is the answer to learning how to be still.

Endnotes

1. Boyd K. Packer, "Do Not Fear," *Ensign*, May 2004, 79.

2. Henry B. Eyring, "Moral Courage," *Ensign*, March 2010, 4.

3. *True to the Faith*, "Sacrament," 148; emphasis added.

4. Dallin H. Oaks, "Your Sacred Duty," *New Era*, May 1999, 4; emphasis added.

5. L. Tom Perry, "The Sabbath and the Sacrament," *Ensign*, May 2011, 8; emphasis added.

6. M. Russell Ballard, "Go for It!" *New Era*, March 2004, 4; emphasis added.

7. See Meredith Willson and Franklin Lacey, *The Music Man* (1957).

8. Richard G. Scott, "Peace of Conscience and Peace of Mind," *Ensign*, Nov. 2004, 18.

9. Bible Dictionary, "Repentance," 760.

10. Ibid., "Pharisees," 750.

11. Gerald N. Lund, *Hearing the Voice of the Lord: Principles and Patterns of Personal Revelation* (Salt Lake City: Deseret Book, 2007), 223–224.

12. Lynn G. Robbins, "What Manner of Men and Women Ought Ye To Be?" *Ensign*, May 2011, 105.

13. Thomas S. Monson, "Finding Joy in the Journey," *Ensign*, Nov. 2008, 85; emphasis added.

14. Ibid., 85–86; emphasis added.

15. Dieter F. Uchtdorf, "Of Things That Matter Most," *Ensign*, Nov. 2010, 22; emphasis added.

16. Richard G. Scott, "The Eternal Blessings of Marriage," *Ensign*, May 2011, 94–95.

17. David A. Bednar, "And Nothing Shall Offend Them," *Ensign*, Nov. 2006, 91.

18. Quentin L. Cook, "LDS Women Are Incredible!" *Ensign*, May 2011, 19–20.

19. Boyd K. Packer, "Solving Emotional Problems in the Lord's Own Way," *Ensign*, Jan. 2010, 51.

20. Neil L. Andersen, "Preparing the World for the Second Coming," *Ensign*, May 2011, 52.

21. Bible Dictionary, "Grace," 697; emphasis added.

22. Russell M. Nelson, "Perfection Pending," *Ensign*, Nov. 1995, 86.

23. Ezra Taft Benson, "The Book of Mormon and the Doctrine and Covenants," *Ensign*, May 1987, 85.

24. Jeffrey R. Holland, "Broken Things to Mend," *Ensign*, May 2006, 70.

25. Jeffrey R. Holland, "Prophets in the Land Again," *Ensign*, Nov. 2006, 106–107.

26. Bruce R. McConkie, "The Probationary Test of Mortality," devotional address, Salt Lake Institute of Religion, University of Utah, Jan. 10, 1982, 8–9; emphasis added.

27. Dieter F. Uchtdorf, "Lift Where You Stand," *Liahona*, Nov. 2008, 54–55, 56.

28. Ibid., 54.

29. Gordon B. Hinckley, "Gambling," *Ensign*, May 2005, 58; emphasis added.

30. Dieter F. Uchtdorf, "Pride and the Priesthood," *Ensign*, Nov. 2010, 58.

31. Joseph Smith Jr., *History of the Church*, 4:597.

32. Boyd K. Packer, "Guided by the Holy Spirit," *Ensign*, May 2011, 30.

33. Richard G. Scott, "To Acquire Spiritual Guidance," *Ensign*, Nov. 2009, 6, 7.

34. Joseph B. Wirthlin, "Come What May, and Love It," *Ensign*, Nov. 2008, 26–27; emphasis added.

35. Ibid., 27.

36. Thomas S. Monson, "Goal beyond Victory," *Ensign*, Nov. 1988, https://www.lds.org/general-conference/1988/10/goal-beyond-victory?lang=eng.

37. Ezra Taft Benson, "Beware of Pride," *Ensign*, May 1989, https://www.lds.org/ensign/1989/05/beware-of-pride?lang=eng.

38. Dieter F. Utchdorf, "Pride and the Priesthood," *Ensign*, Nov. 2010, 56.

39. Bible Dictionary, 762.

40. *Hymns*, no. 124.

41. Bruce C. Hafen, *A Disciple's Life: The Biography of Elder Neal A. Maxwell* (Salt Lake City: Deseret Book, 2002), 550; emphasis added.

42. "I Know That My Redeemer Lives," *Hymns*, no. 136.

About the Author

G. Sheldon Martin is a seminary teacher and a Clinical Mental Health Counselor. He grew up in Palmdale, California; attended Ricks College and BYU; and served a mission to Paris, France. He is a favorite speaker at Education Week, EFY, and youth conferences around the country. With a master's degree in mental health counseling, he specializes in the areas of parenting, marriage, anxiety, depression, pornography addiction, and struggling teens. He and his wife, Nicole, are the parents of five children. He is currently serving as bishop of his ward.